THE TRAMP'S ANTHOLOGY

*A recipe: All these go to the making of good
tramper's coffee.*

THE TRAMP'S ANTHOLOGY

Edited by

STEPHEN GRAHAM

LONDON: PETER DAVIES

1928

You shall be all by yourself in the midst of the world and the Divine picture-book shall be put in your hands for you to open.

Pages 205-6

Printed in Great Britain

THE LITERATURE OF WALKING

Walking is close to reading and writing. We have seen more by the midday sun than by midnight oil. Our walks have begotten our thoughts. Words, sentences, books and poems are associated with our walking. The mind fructifies under the influence of walking : that is why we word-workers, when we cannot see clearly the way from sentence to sentence in our writing, get up and pace the room. Or, casting a glance at the sky " vainly sweet," we throw down our pens and plunge outward by hedge-row and thicket over the fields to the high woods. The characteristic literary man living in the country writes in the morning, walks all the afternoon. Or he walks till noon and writes half an hour before lunch. On such occasions he sometimes writes all through lunch with a writing-pad where his bread-plate ought to be. I have written a good deal myself while actually walking, walking and writing at the same time as I go along a road. Forty thousand words of one of my Sketches were written in that way. God gives us a third eye for the scenery. Reading and walking at the same time is perhaps not so defensible, and yet with what added pleasure one reads a book that one takes out into the air. I once tramped across Yorkshire reading Joseph Andrews, and at least felt nearer to Parson Adams and the England of the time.

The inventors of comfortable chairs have done some disservice to humanity, giving a false importance and consideration to our hips which in this generation are, I am sure, exaggerated. We do too much sitting down, spend too much time in libraries, studies, and museums. A very popular, but over-bookish writer has said that before ever he began to write he spent five years in the British Museum—" And oh! the difference to me: the difference to my readers! " But this is a false scent: Psyche is not in Bloomsbury.

A man once explained himself to me in these terms:

" What are you doing now? " I asked.

"Oh, I spend eight hours a day in the British Museum. I am mugging up a subject to write a book."

One knows the sort of book—" mugged up," written for " mugs." But you cannot mug up life.

The best of our literature has open-air inspiration. One feels that Wordsworth is walking all the time, and that even now in his heaven, wherever it may be, he is still remarking some primrose by the river's brim. Richard Jefferies is just walking made perfect and transmuted to prose. All southern Scotland marches through the works of Walter Scott—" All the blue bonnets are over the Border." Carlyle was more of a walker and an open-air man when he wrote Sartor Resartus *than when he wrote* Frederick the Great. *He was a great museum worker, but, finding the dead, he lost the living. Ruskin, wherever he might be found, at Oxford or in Westmoreland or in Italy, was wedded in deep love to God's creation. Thence came his primary inspiration. He was only secondarily moved by the work of men's hands.*

Walking has been so natural and so ordinary that few thought of writing about it. Chaucer and Shakespeare walked a-plenty; a sparkling out-of-doors England rules over their writing like a summer sky over a festival. It is only in this age, as a protest against the wheel, walking as a literary cult has come into being. The pioneer seems to have been the Rev. A. N. Cooper, rector of Filey, who astonished his parishioners by walking to Rome in a month. Not only did he walk across Western Europe, but walked first from his vicarage the length of England to a southern port. Then he tramped across Ireland, across Denmark, across Scandinavia, and I know not what other countries, and wrote some interesting books on his adventures. He was followed by Hilaire Belloc who, as a gesture, walked also to Rome and recorded his adventure with much literary grace. It was from Belloc that the younger generation caught the idea that walking was possible.

Then in Russia there appeared a great tramp writer, Maxim Gorky. It should be remarked that although the upper classes in Russia cannot walk, the peasantry are the greatest walkers in Europe. And the country swarms with tramps, vagabonds, and pilgrims. Gorky was typical of Russia in his way of life, though very remarkable as a writer. He was uneducated, penniless, more or less a ragamuffin, and yet he wrote some books which will undoubtedly be considered part of the lasting literature of Russia. I refer to his fresh early works, such as Foma Gordyef, Three, The Fellow-Traveller. Later, when he tucked in his shirt and became middle-class, his genius failed him. Probably there is not a better tramping story than The Fellow-Traveller in literature.

Gorky, translated into English, gave a turn to walking as a literary cult, and made tramping and vagabondage more possible. This was strengthened by the discovery of W. H. Davies, an actual hobo, one of the swarm of tramps in America in the great immigration period, the only one, perhaps, to raise a head and burst into self-expression. The Autobiography of a Super-Tramp was more remarkable at the time it appeared than it seems now. That is because having got the seed the flower can be grown.

Edward Thomas carried on the walking cult, but his literary promise was unfortunately removed by death in the war.

In America, walking as a stunt had long since made its appearance, and had been exploited journalistically. Scores of men and some women have done the long tramp from Atlantic to Pacific—and if they have not themselves written about it, have at least been written up. Occasionally such a volume as The Adventures of a Scholar-Tramp, *by Glen Mullin, has appeared, a remarkable picture of the American vagrant, who " steps " trains and " batters " for bread.*

The inspiration of Walt Whitman, who was a great walker, has not been constant in the country where the motto was invented: " Why walk when you can ride? " and yet Vachel Lindsay is directly in his tradition, and his tramping and " singing " are memorable in contemporary American life.

America also produced Jack London, who was not quite so much of a tramp and vagabond as Gorky. A gifted and interesting writer, but I do not feel that he knew a great deal about tramping. The adventures of the man and his wife tramping in The Valley of the Moon *hardly correspond to reality. But Jack London helped to make literary tramps.*

Personally, I wish there were more literary tramps. Young people come to me and say: " How shall I write?" and I generally answer: " First you must live." Books should not beget books; life should beget books. Tramping and vagabondage is a short cut to reality. It is the same now as in the fourteenth century when some unknown tramp could write—

Thus I, Colin Clout,
As I go about
And wondering as I walk
I hear the people talk.

Men say for silver and gold
Mitres are bought and sold.
A straw for Goddys curse
What are they the worse?
What care the clergy though Gill sweat
Or Jack of the Noke?

and the rest. Wondering as I walk I hear the people talk. That is a great part of the literature of walking.

Still we must not forget walking is a quiet joy and can be its own reward. Walking is part of health and happiness. Thank God for thy feet! My object in compiling this book is—

As a bird each fond endearment tries
To tempt its new-fledged offspring to the skies—

well, just that—to tempt you to take up your heavy solid boots and say: " I will not waste this day; I will not even sit down reading this anthology, but put it in my pocket and take it out when lark song is in my ears."

STEPHEN GRAHAM

ACKNOWLEDGMENT

MR. STEPHEN GRAHAM is indebted to the following publishers and authors (or their literary executors) for their permission to use copyright work in this book, and is very grateful to those whose generosity has enabled him to include so much of it:

ALLEN AND UNWIN: The Open Secret (Towards Democracy), *Edward Carpenter*.

ALLEN AND UNWIN: I wandered down the Mountain (The Path to Rome), *Hilaire Belloc*.

ERNEST BENN, LTD.: Francks' Beginning, In Honduras, *Harry A. Franck*.

ERNEST BENN, LTD.: A Holiday on Tramp, The Road to Rome (Road to Rome), *A. N. Cooper*.

ARNOLD BENNETT, ESQ.: A Man may Desire to go to Mecca (Twenty-Four Hours a Day), *A. Bennett*.

WM. BLACKWOOD AND SONS, LTD.: The Lost Pibroch, *Neil Munro*.

BRENTANO'S, LTD.: Emblems of Tramping (Gentle Art of Tramping), *Stephen Graham*.

J. CAPE, LTD.: Davies loses his Leg (Autobiography of a Super Tramp), *W. H. Davies*.

CASSELL AND CO., LTD.: Central Asian Stars (Through Central Asia), *Stephen Graham*.

CHATTO AND WINDUS: Why do you go the same Road every Day? (The Open Air), *Richard Jefferies*.

CONSTABLE AND CO., LTD.: Earth's Secret, *George Meredith*.

DE LA MORE PRESS: The Jumping-off Place, Lying Awake at Night (The Forest), *Stewart E. White*.

J. M. DENT AND SONS, LTD.: Hudson and his Wife Afoot, Bare Feet, *W. H. Hudson*.

G. DUCKWORTH AND CO., LTD.: In every little blade of grass beats the heart (Prince Shakro), *Maxim Gorky*.

EXECUTORS OF RUPERT BROOKE: The Old Vicarage, Grantchester (Collected Poems), *Rupert Brooke*.

GERALD GOULD, ESQ.: Wander-thirst, *Gerald Gould*.

WILLIAM HEINEMANN, LTD.: From Larissa (A Three-legged Tour), *Dame Ethel Smythe*.

HODDER AND STOUGHTON: Mistle Thrushes, Starlings, Bullfinches, Blackbirds, Nightingales, and Robins (The Charm of Birds), *Viscount Grey of Fallodon*.

W. G. HOLE, ESQ.: Along and Down Along, *W. G. Hole*.

JACKSON, WYLIE AND CO.: Footpaths, *Canon Rawnsley*.

RUDYARD KIPLING, ESQ.: The Explorer, The Feet of the Young Men (The Five Nations), The Song of the Banjo (The Seven Seas), *Rudyard Kipling*.

JOHN LANE THE BODLEY HEAD, LTD.: Lapland (Two Vagabonds in Sweden and Lapland), *Jan and Cora Gordon*.

JOHN LANE THE BODLEY HEAD, LTD.: Dawn in the Caucasus (A Vagabond in the Caucasus), *Stephen Graham*.

JOHN LONG, LTD.: Open Air! (A Tramp's Philosophy), *Bart Kennedy*.

MACMILLAN AND CO., LTD.: The Scots Guards Enter Germany (A Private in the Guards), *Stephen Graham*.

MACMILLAN AND CO., LTD.: In Quest of El Dorado (The Band at Oaxaca, Southern Mexico), *Stephen Graham*.

MACMILLAN AND CO., LTD.: Farewell to the Town (In Quest of El Dorado), *Stephen Graham*.

MACMILLAN AND CO., LTD.: Climbing a Peak in Darien (In Quest of El Dorado), *Stephen Graham*.

MACMILLAN AND CO., LTD.: The Great Divide (Tramping with a Poet in the Rockies), *Stephen Graham*.

THE MACMILLAN COMPANY: The Santa-Fe Trail (The Santa-Fe Trail), *Vachel Lindsay*.

THE MACMILLAN COMPANY: Rules of the Road, *Vachel Lindsay*.

THE MACMILLAN COMPANY: Gospel of Beachcombing, *Vachel Lindsay*.

THE MACMILLAN COMPANY: Mystic Uniform of the Mountain Sunset, *Vachel Lindsay*.

THE MACMILLAN COMPANY: Oh, I have walked in Kansas, *Vachel Lindsay*.

ELKIN MATHEWS AND MARROT, LTD.: The Joys of the Road, *Bliss Carman*.

METHUEN AND CO., LTD.: The Explorer, The Feet of the Young Men (The Five Nations), *Rudyard Kipling*.

METHUEN AND CO., LTD.: The Song of the Banjo, The Seven Seas, *Rudyard Kipling*.

DR. NEIL MUNRO: The Lost Pibroch, *Neil Munro*.

CECIL PALMER: Along and Down Along, *W. G. Hole*.

RICHARDS PRESS, LTD.: I felt the world a-spinning on its Nave, *John Davidson*.

CHARLES SCRIBNERS' SONS (New York): Earth's Secret, *George Meredith*.

SIDGWICK AND JACKSON, LTD.: The Old Vicarage, Grantchester (Collected Poems), *Rupert Brooke*.

WELLS GARDNER, DARTON AND CO., LTD.: A Dream ("A Bundle of Memories"), *Henry Scott Holland*.

WILLIAMS AND NORGATE, LTD.: No philosopher has ever had a clearer conception of the true end of man than I had at the age of 12, *Prof. L. P. Jacks*.

ACKNOWLEDGMENT

Mr. STEPHEN GRAHAM is indebted to the following publishers and authors (or their literary executors) for their permission to use copyright work in this book, and is very grateful to those whose generosity has enabled him to include so much of it:

ALLEN AND UNWIN: The Open Secret (Towards Democracy), Edward Carpenter.

ALLEN AND UNWIN: I wandered down the Mountain (The Path to Rome), Hilaire Belloc.

ERNEST BENN, LTD.: Francké Beginning, In Honduras Harry A. Franck.

ERNEST BENN, LTD.: A Holiday on Tramp, The Road to Rome (Road to Rome), A. N. Cooper.

ARNOLD BENNETT, ESQ.: A Man may Desire to go to Mecca (Twenty Four Hours a Day), A. Bennett.

WM. BLACKWOOD AND SONS, LTD.: The Lost Pibroch, Neil Munro.

BENTRAND'S, LTD.: Emblems of Tramping (Gentle Art of Tramping), Stephen Graham.

J. CAPE, LTD.: Davies loses his Leg (Autobiography of a Super Tramp), W. H. Davies.

CASSELL AND CO., LTD.: Central Asian Stars (Through Central Asia), Stephen Graham.

CHATTO AND WINDUS: Why do you go the same Road every Day? (The Open Air), Richard Jefferies.

CONSTABLE AND CO., LTD.: Earth's Secret, George Meredith.

DE LA MORE PRESS: The Jumping-off Place, Living Awake at Night (The Forest), Stewart E. White.

xiii

I: MORNING

Awake! for Morning in the Bowl of Night
Has flung the Stone that puts the Stars to Flight:
   And Lo! the Hunter of the East has caught
The Sultan's Turret in a Noose of Light.

Omar Khayyám

II: EVENING

   For note, when evening shuts,
      A certain moment cuts
The deed off, calls the glory from the grey:
      A whisper from the west
      Shoots—" Add this to the rest,
" Take it and try its worth! here dies another day."

Robert Browning

III: THE VISION

I am a wanderer, I remember well
One journey, how I feared the track was missed
So long the city I desired to reach
Lay hid; when suddenly its spires afar
Flashed through the circling clouds; conceive my joy!
Too soon the vapours closed o'er it again,
But I had seen the city, and one such glance
No darkness could obscure:

.   .   .   .   .

I

B

How know I else such glorious fate my own,
But in the restless irresistible force
That works within me? Is it for human will
To institute such impulses?—still less
To disregard their promptings? What should I
Do, kept among you all; your loves, your cares,
Your life—all to be mine? Be sure that God
Ne'er dooms to waste the strength he deigns impart!
Ask the gier-eagle why she stoops at once
Into the vast and unexplored abyss,
What full-grown power informs her from the first,
Why she not marvels, strenuously beating
The silent boundless regions of the sky!

Robert Browning

IV

A fool sees not the same tree that a wise man sees.
He whose face gives no light shall never become a star.

William Blake

V

. . . a voice, as bad as Conscience, rang interminable
    changes
On one everlasting Whisper day and night repeated
    —so:
" Something hidden. Go and find it. Go and look
    behind the ranges—
" Something lost behind the Ranges. Lost and wait-
    ing for you. Go! "

.   .   .   .   .

Yes, your " Never-never-couutry "—yes, your " edge
of cultivation "
And " no sense in going further "—till I crossed the
range to see.

.   .   .   .   .

Anybody might have found it, but—His Whisper
came to Me!

Rudyard Kipling

VI

Life is sweet, brother . . . There's day and
night, brother, both sweet things; sun, moon, and
stars, all sweet things; there's likewise a wind on
the heath.

George Borrow

VII: UNDER THE GREENWOOD TREE

Under the greenwood tree
Who loves to lie with me,
And tune his merry note
Unto the sweet bird's throat,
Come hither, come hither, come hither:
Here shall he see
No enemy
But winter and rough weather.

Who doth ambition shun
And loves to live i' the sun,
Seeking the food he eats
And pleased with what he gets,

3

Come hither, come hither, come hither:
   Here shall he see
   No enemy
But winter and rough weather.

   If it do come to pass
   That any man turn ass,
   Leaving his wealth and ease,
   A stubborn will to please,
Ducdame, ducdame, ducdame:
   Here shall he see
   Gross fools as he,
An if he will come to me.

.   .   .   .   .   .

Call me not fool till heaven hath sent me fortune.
William Shakespeare

VIII

In every little blade of grass beats the heart of the
Lord; every insect of the air or of the earth breathes
his Holy Spirit; everywhere the Lord God Jesus
Christ is living! What beauty there is upon the earth,
in the fields, and in the forests! Have you ever been
on the Kerzhentz? There is a calm there which cannot be compared, in the trees, in the grass—heavenly
. . .

You look up at the sky, lying somewhere under a
little bush, and it seems to be descending to you as if
it wished to embrace you . . . the soul is warm and
quietly joyful; you ask nothing of anyone, you envy
nobody. . . . So it seems as if in all the world—there
were only you and God. . . .   *Maxim Gorky*

4

IX

I walked without aim through woods, through valleys, and over brooks and through sleeping villages, to enjoy the great Night, like a day. I walked and still looked, like the magnet, to the region of midnight, to strengthen my heart at the gleaming twilight, at this up-stretching Aurora of a morning beneath our feet. White night-butterflies flitted, white blossoms fluttered, white stars fell, and the white snow powder hung silvery in the high Shadow of the Earth, which reaches beyond the moon, and which is our Night. Then began the Aeolian Harp of the Creation to tremble and to sound, blown on from above; and my immortal soul was a string in that Harp . . . the distant village clock struck midnight, mingling as it were with the ever-pealing tone of ancient Eternity.

Jean Paul Richter

X

An irresistible desire seized him to bathe; he undressed himself and stepped into the basin. He felt as if a sunset cloud were floating around him; a heavenly emotion streamed over his soul; in deep pleasure innumerable thoughts strove to blend within him; new unseen images arose . . . every wave of that soft element pressed itself on him like a soft bosom. The flood seemed a Spirit of Beauty which from moment to moment was taking form round the youth.

Novalis

XI: THE SONG OF THE OPEN ROAD

Afoot and light-hearted I take to the open road,
Healthy, free, the world before me,
The long brown path before me leading wherever I
    choose.

Henceforth I ask not good-fortune, I myself am good-
    fortune,
Henceforth I whimper no more, postpone no more,
    need nothing,
Done with indoor complaints, libraries, querulous
    criticisms,
Strong and content I travel the open road.

The earth, that is sufficient,
I do not want the constellations any nearer,
I know they are very well where they are,
I know they suffice for those who belong to them.

.   .   .   .   .   .

You road I enter upon and look around, I believe you
    are not all that is here,
I believe that much unseen is also here.

Here the profound lesson of reception, nor preference
    nor denial,
The black with his woolly head, the felon, the diseas'd,
    the illiterate person, are not denied;
The birth, the hasting after the physician, the beggar's
    tramp, the drunkard's stagger, the laughing party
    of mechanics,
The escaped youth, the rich person's carriage, the fop,
    the eloping couple,

The early market-man, the hearse, the moving of
    furniture into the town, the return back from the
    town,
They pass, I also pass, anything passes, none can be
    interdicted.
None but are accepted, none but shall be dear to me.

. . . . .

The earth expanding right hand and left hand,
The picture alive, each part in its best light,
The music falling in where it is wanted, and stopping
    where it is not wanted,
The cheerful voice of the public road, the gay fresh
    sentiment of the road.

O highway I travel, do you say to me *Do not leave me?*
Do you say *Venture not—if you leave me you are lost?*
Do you say *I am already prepared, I am well-beaten
    and undenied, adhere to me?*

O public road, I say back I am not afraid to leave you,
    yet I love you,
You express me better than I can express myself,
You shall be more to me than my poem.

I think heroic deeds were all conceived in the open
    air, and all free poems also,
I think I could stop here myself and do miracles,
I think whatever I shall meet on the road I shall like,
    and whoever beholds me shall like me,
I think whoever I see must be happy.

7

From this hour I ordain myself loos'd of limits and
  imaginary lines,
Going where I list, my own master total and absolute,
Listening to others, considering well what they say,
Pausing, searching, receiving, contemplating,
Gently, but with undeniable will, divesting myself of
  the holds that would hold me.

I inhale great draughts of space,
The east and the west are mine, and the north and the
  south are mine.
I am larger, better than I thought,
I did not know I held so much goodness.

All seems beautiful to me,
I can repeat over to men and women You have done
  such good to me I would do the same to you,
I will recruit for myself and you as I go,
I will scatter myself among men and women as I go,
I will toss a new gladness and roughness among them,
Whoever denies me it shall not trouble me,
Whoever accepts me he or she shall be blessed and
  shall bless me.

Now if a thousand perfect men were to appear it
  would not amaze me,
Now if a thousand beautiful forms of women appear'd
  it would not astonish me.
Now I see the secret of the making of the best persons,
It is to grow in the open air and to eat and sleep with
  the earth.

. . . .

Allons! after the great Companions, and to belong to
   them!
They too are on the road—they are the swift and
   majestic men—they are the greatest women,
Enjoyers of calms of seas and storms of seas,
Sailors of many a ship, walkers of many a mile of land,
Habitués of many distant countries, habitués of far-
   distant dwellings,
Trusters of men and women, observers of cities,
   solitary toilers,
Pausers and contemplators of tufts, blossoms, shells
   of the shore,
Dancers at wedding-dances, kissers of brides, tender
   helpers of children, bearers of children,
Soldiers of revolts, standers by gaping graves, lowerers
   down of coffins,
Journeyers over consecutive seasons, over the years,
   the curious years each emerging from that which
   preceded it,
Journeyers as with companions, namely their own
   diverse phrases,
Forth-steppers from the latent unrealised baby-days,
Journeyers gaily with their own youth, journeyers with
   their bearded and well-grain'd manhood,
Journeyers with their womanhood, ample, unsur-
   passed, content,
Journeyers with their own sublime old age of manhood or womanhood,
Old age, calm, expanded, broad with the haughty
   breadth of the universe,
Old age, flowing free with the delicious near-by free-
   dom of death.

Allons! to that which is endless as it was beginning-
     less,
To undergo much, tramps of days, rests of nights,
To merge all in the travel they tend to, and the days
     and nights they tend to,
Again to merge them in the start of superior journeys,
To see nothing anywhere but what you may reach it
     and pass it,
To conceive no time, however distant, but what you
     may reach it and pass it,
To look up or down no road but it stretches and waits
     for you, however long but it stretches and waits
     for you,
To see no being, not God's or any, but you also go
     thither,
To see no possession but you may possess it, enjoying
     all without labour of purchase, abstracting the
     feast yet not abstracting one particle of it,
To take the best of the farmer's farm and the rich
     man's elegant villa, and the chaste blessings of
the well-married couple, and the fruits of orchards
     and flowers of gardens,
To take to your use out of the compact cities as you
     pass through,
To carry buildings and streets with you afterward
     wherever you go,
To gather the minds of men out of their brains as you
     encounter them, to gather the love out of their
     hearts,
To take your lovers on the road with you, for all that
     you leave them behind you,
To know the universe itself as a road, as many roads,
     as roads for travelling souls.

.   .   .   .   .

Allons! the road is before us!

It is safe—I have tried it—my own feet have tried it well—be not detain'd!

Let the paper remain on the desk unwritten, and the book on the shelf unopen'd!

Let the tools remain in the workshop! let the money remain unearn'd!

Let the school stand! mind not the cry of the teacher!

Let the preacher preach in his pulpit! let the lawyer plead in the court, and the judge expound the law.

Camerado, I give you my hand!

I give you my love more precious than money,

I give you myself before preaching or law;

Will you give me yourself? will you come travel with me?

Shall we stick by each other as long as we live?

Walt Whitman

XII

He who has been born has been a First Man; has had lying before his young eyes and as yet unharnessed into scientific shapes, a world as elastic, infinite, divine, as lay before the eyes of Adam himself.

.　　.　　.　　.

I look up to the everlasting sky, and with the azure infinitude all around me cannot think that I was made in vain.

Thomas Carlyle

XIII

WHAN that Aprille with his shoures soote
The droghte of March hath perced to the roote,
And bathed every veyne in swich licour
Of which vertu engendred is the flour;
When Zephirus eek with his swete breeth
Inspired hath in every holt and heeth
The tendre croppes, and the yonge sonne
Hath in the Ram his halfe cours y-ronne,
And smale foweles maken melodye,
That slepen al the nyght with open eye,—
So priketh hem Nature in hir corages,—
Than longen folk to goon on pilgrimages,
And palmeres to seken straunge strondes
To ferne halwes, kowthe in sondry londes;
And specially, from every shires ende
Of Engelond, to Canterbury they wende,
The hooly blisful martir for to seke
That hem hath holpen whan that they were seeke.

Chaucer

XIV: THE COMING OF SPRING

I heard that a visitor had come. He was waiting in the porch.

I went out and looked. It was a little monk.

" Good day," he said. And then he stared at me seriously, as if he were trying to find out something.

It was a wee monk, all in white.

" Good day! What do you want? "

" Oh nothing," said he. " I'm just going round from house to house." And he handed me a little branch.

" What's that? " said I to him. " You don't mean to say there are leaves on it! "

" Leaves," said the little monk, and smiled.

Then I felt so happy. I didn't know what to do with myself. It seemed as if not only the little twig that he had given me, but the whole room, all the walls and window-frames, had burst into leaves.

" Wouldn't you like a hot biscuit? " said I. " They're cooking them in the kitchen."

" No."

" But have something! A little milk, eh? "

" No."

" Some apples then? "

" Wouldn't mind . . . some honey," said the monk, speaking like a little boy.

When the monk said this I felt as if I remembered something. " Why," said I, " I've seen you before somewhere, haven't I? "

The little monk smiled.

And there I stood on the threshold and looked out into the garden. I held the little branch tightly, and its tiny leaves all looked out to the sun. And it was mine, my very own.

The little monk stood there smiling.

Alexei Remizof

XV

The year's at the spring,
And day's at the morn:
Morning's at seven;
The hill-side's dew-pearled;

The lark's on the wing;
The snail's on the thorn;
God's in his heaven—
All's right with the world.

Robert Browning

XVI

Every day is a sun-ray.

Schopenhauer

XVII: THE JUMPING-OFF PLACE

Sometime, no matter how long your journey, you will reach a spot whose psychological effect is so exactly like a dozen others that you will recognise at once its kinship with former experience. Mere physical likeness does not count at all. It may possess a water-front of laths and sawdust, or an outlook over broad, shimmering, heat-baked plains. It may front the impassive fringe of a forest, or it may skirt the calm stretch of a river. But whether of log or mud, stone or unpainted board, its identity becomes at first sight indubitably evident. Were you, by the wave of some beneficent wand, to be transported direct to it from the heart of the city, you could not fail to recognise it. " The jumping-off place! " you would cry ecstatically.

For here is where begins the Long Trail. Whether it will lead you through the forests, or up the hills, or over the plains, or by invisible water-paths; whether you will accomplish it on horseback, or in canoe, or by the transportation of your own two legs; whether your companions shall be white or red, or merely the voices of the wilds—these things matter not a particle. In the symbol of this little town you loose your hold on the world of made things, and shift for yourself among the unchanging conditions of nature.

Here the faint forest flavour, the subtle, invisible breath of freedom, stirs faintly across men's conventions. The ordinary affairs of life savour of this tang— a trace of wildness in the domesticated berry. In the dress of the inhabitants is a dash of colour, a carelessness of port; in the manner of their greeting is the clear, steady-eyed taciturnity of the silent places; through the web of their grey talk of ways and means and men's simpler beliefs runs a thread of colour. One hears strange, suggestive words and phrases—arapajo, capote, arroyo, the diamond hitch, cache, butte, coule, muskegs, portage, and a dozen others coined into the tender of daily use. And occasionally, when the expectation is least alert, one encounters suddenly the very symbol of the wilderness itself—a dust-whitened cowboy, an Indian packer with his straight, fillet-confined hair, a voyageur gay in red sash and ornamented moccasins, one of the Company's canoemen, hollow-cheeked from the river—no costumed show exhibit, but fitting naturally into the scene, bringing something of the open space with him so that in your imagination the little town gradually takes on the colour of mystery which an older community utterly lacks.

Stewart E. White

16

XVIII: IN THE FOREST

And foorth they passe, with pleasure forward led,
Joying to heare the birdes sweete harmony,
Which, therein shrouded from the tempest dred,
Seemd in their song to scorne the cruell sky.
Much can they praise the trees so straight and hy,
The sayling Pine; the Cedar proud and tall;
The vine-propp Elme; the Poplar never dry;
The builder Oake, sole king of forrests all;
The Aspine good for staves; the Cypresse funerall;

The Laurell, meed of mightie Conquerours
And Poets sage; the Firre that weepeth still;
The Willow, worne of forlorne Paramours;
The Eugh, obedient to the benders will;
The Birch for shaftes; the Sallow for the mill;
The Mirrhe-sweete-bleeding in the bitter wound;
The warlike Beech; the Ash for nothing ill;
The fruitfull Olive; and the Platane round;
The carver Holme; the Maple seeldom inward sound.

Led with delight, they thus beguile the way.

Edmund Spenser

XIX: FAREWELL TO THE TOWN

The town is one large house of which all the little
houses are rooms. The streets are the stairs. Those
who live always in the town never go out of doors
even if they do take the air in the streets.

When I came into the town I found that in my
soul were reflected its blank walls, its interminable
stairways, and its shadows of hurrying traffic.

C

A thousand sights and impressions, unbidden, unwelcome, flooded through the eye-gate of my soul, and a thousand harsh sounds and noises came to me through my ears and echoed within me. I became aware of confused influences of all kinds striving to find some habitation in the temple of my being.

What had been my delight in the country, my receptivity and hospitality of consciousness, became in the town my misery and my despair.

For imagine! Within my own calm mirror a beautiful world had seen itself rebuilded. Mountains and valleys lay within me, robed in sunny and cloudy days or marching in the majesty of storm. I had inbreathed their mystery and outbreathed it again as my own. I had gazed at the wide foaming seas till they had gazed into me, and all their waves waved their proud crests within me. Beauteous plains had tempted, mysterious dark forests lured me, and I had loved them and given them habitation in my being. My soul had been wedded to the great strong sun and it had slumbered under the watchful stars.

The silence of vast lonely places was preserved in my breast. Or against the background of that silence resounded in my being the roar of the billows of the ocean. Great woods roared about my mountains, or the whispering snow hurried over them as over tents. In my valleys I heard the sound of rivulets; in my forests the birds. Choirs of birds sang within my breast. I had been a play-fellow with God. God had played with me as with a child.

Bound by so intimate a tie, how terrible to have been betrayed to a town!

For now, fain would the evil city reflect itself in my calm soul, its commerce take up a place within the

18

temple of my being. I had left God's handiwork and come to the man-made town. I had left the inexplicable and come to the realm of the explained. In the holy temple were arcades of shops; through its precincts hurried the trams; the pictures of trade were displayed; men were building hoardings in my soul and posting notices of idol-worship, and hurrying throngs were reading books of the rites of idolatry. Instead of the mighty anthem of the ocean I heard the roar of traffic. Where had been mysterious forests now stood dark chimneys, and the songs of birds were exchanged for the shrill whistle of trains.

And my being began to express itself to itself in terms of commerce.

" Oh God," I cried in my sorrow, " who did play with me among the mountains, refurnish my soul! Purge Thy Temple as Thou didst in Jerusalem of old time, when Thou didst overset the tables of the money-changers."

Then the spirit drove me into the wilderness to my mountains and valleys, by the side of the great sea and by the haunted forests. Once more the vast dome of heaven became the roof of my house, and within the house was rebuilded that which my soul called beautiful. There I refound my God, and my being re-expressed itself to itself in terms of eternal Mysteries. I vowed I should never again belong to the town.

As upon a spring day the face of heaven is hid and a storm descends, winds ruffle the bosom of a pure lake, the flowers droop, wet, the birds cease singing, and rain rushes over all, and then anon the face of heaven clears, the sun shines forth, the flowers look up in tears, the birds sing again, and the pure lake reflects once more the pure depth of the sky, so now

my glad soul, which had lost its sun, found it again,
and remembered its birds and its flowers.

Stephen Graham

XX: ORISON

Give to me the free life,
　　Fresh air, and laughter,
Let all the world go hang
　　For what comes after.
Give me the song, the dream
　　On love's lips singing,
The blue sky, the lark's way
　　At Heaven's gates swinging.

Give me the white, the winding road
　　In June's Sun shining,
A cooling dip in silver streams
　　The red roses lining;
A thatched cottage under the hill
　　At gay sun-setting,
A deep sleep when all is done,
　　And the long forgetting.

Henry Simpson

XXI

Oh! that the Desert were my dwelling-place,
With one fair Spirit for my minister,
That I might all forget the human race,
And, hating no one, love but only her!
Ye elements!—in whose ennobling stir
I feel myself exalted—Can ye not
Accord me such a being? Do I err
In deeming such inhabit many a spot?
Though with them to converse can rarely be our lot.

There is a pleasure in the pathless woods,
There is a rapture in the lonely shore,
There is society, where none intrudes,
By the deep Sea, and music in its roar:
I love not man the less, but Nature more.
From these our interviews, in which I steal
From all I may be, or have been before,
To mingle with the Universe, and feel
What I can ne'er express, yet cannot all conceal.

Byron

XXII

A Book of Verses underneath the Bough,
A Jug of Wine, a Loaf of Bread—and Thou
Beside me singing in the Wilderness—
O, Wilderness were Paradise enow!

Omar Khayyám

XXIII

To one who has been long in city pent,
   'Tis very sweet to look into the fair
   And open face of heaven,—to breathe a prayer
Full in the smile of the blue firmament.
Who is more happy, when, with hearts content,
   Fatigued he sinks into some pleasant lair
   Of wavy grass and reads a debonair
And gentle tale of love and languishment?

Returning home at evening, with an ear
    Catching the notes of Philomel,—an eye
Watching the sailing cloudlet's bright career,
    He mourns that day so soon has glided by:
E'en like the passage of an angel's tear
    That falls through the clear ether silently.

John Keats

XXIV: THE SKYLARK

Bird of the wilderness,
Blithesome and cumberless,
Sweet be thy matin o'er moorland and lea!
    Emblem of happiness,
    Blest is thy dwelling-place—
Oh, to abide in the desert with thee!

Wild is thy lay, and loud,
Far in the downy cloud,
Love gives it energy; love gave it birth.
    Where, on thy dewy wing,
    Where art thou journeying?
Thy lay is in heaven, thy love is on earth.

O'er fell and fountain sheen,
O'er moor and mountain green,
O'er the red streamer that heralds the day,
    Over the cloudlet dim,
    Over the rainbow's rim,
Musical cherub, soar, singing, away.

Then, when the gloaming comes,
Low in the heather blooms
Sweet will thy welcome and bed of love be.
   Emblem of happiness,
   Blest is thy dwelling place,
Oh, to abide in the desert with thee!

James Hogg

XXV: THE CHARM OF BIRDS

1. *Mistle-thrushes.*

The mistle-thrush is best appreciated in January and February. Not that he sings better then than later on; indeed his song is more perfect in April, but it is very good in the two first months of the year, and it stands out clear in the then comparatively silent air. There are boldness and wildness as well as sweetness in the tone. It has not the rich and moving quality of the blackbird and yet it stirs us. For on a windy day in January, when the blackbirds seek the shelter of laurels and thickets and have not a note of song in them, the mistle-thrush sings, aloft and conspicuous. There is, it has been well said, " weather in his song." Birds as a rule seem to dislike wind more than any other sort of weather, but the mistle-thrush is less discomfited by it than any other song-bird. On a windy day early in the year the " storm-cock " will mount his tree, and there in full exposure proclaim by song that he is vigorous and glad. Every year he deserves to be honourably and gratefully saluted.

2. *Starlings.*

. . . the starling. His song (for his very musical performance must be given that name) has been heard all through the autumn. When thrushes do not sing it is the most valuable and conspicuous event in bird music during the autumn and winter; every evening about sunset a starling, or a little party of them, sits on the top of a bare tree and gives a variety performance; some notes are their own, others are plagiarisms more or less close to the original; some are perfect imitations. The note that seems to me to be peculiarly the starling's own is a very clear boyish whistle; with this are all manner of other sounds—poultry noises, the chatter of sparrows, the cry of a peewit—one never knows what is coming next. Some of the notes are very pleasant, even beautiful, and are a delight to hear. The starling cannot attain to the quality of a blackbird, but he can whistle so near to it that more than once in February have I stopped and listened, thinking that I had heard all unawares the first blackbird, till some chatter or chuckling satisfied me that it was only part of the starling's infinite variety. Where curlews breed, the spring notes of the curlew are a very favourite imitation. Nobody but a curlew can make that wonderful sound; but this does not deter the starling from attempting it, and the resemblance of the imitation to the original is sufficient to make us thank him. The starling is like a gramophone among bird songs, and it has chosen some of the best of which to make records.

3. *Chaffinches.*

His song is robust and buoyant. Warde Fowler gives a very apt description of it in one of his books. He compares the manner of it to a bowler running with quick steps up to the wicket, and then with an overhand turn of the arm delivering the ball; and he notes that when the chaffinch first begins to sing it cannot for some days " deliver the ball " ; it gets to the wicket and stops. To those who know the song this illustration will surely commend itself. I have known people complain of the persistent iteration of the chaffinch's song, and I must admit that it does suggest a happiness that is a little trivial and commonplace. If the chaffinch were human, one can imagine that he would say " Cheerio! " as a greeting to a friend. It is pleasant to play with these criticisms of a chaffinch; to do so, when one had a sure affection for it, does not really lessen one's feeling for the song, but endears it. The song is so persistent and abundant, that from February well on into June it is a commonplace in the bird chorus; and yet one chaffinch stands out in my memory as does a single dipper and a single wren. It was in the Whitsuntide recess, when for a few precious days late in May or early in June, I had escaped from Parliament and from London, whose " season " then is so miserably unseasonable. The days were fine and bright. On a stone coping of a little parapet, that went round the roof at Fallodon, at a corner that faced due south, a chaffinch used to take its stand, and from that eminence day after day it pelted me with song whenever I went on the lawn outside. This one bird became a feature of the holiday, an embodiment of happiness proclaimed from the house-top. Wordsworth, in memory of a day spent by " a little unpretending rill," says:

" The immortal spirit of one happy day
    Lingers beside that rill in vision clear;"

and for me the immortal spirit of those happy Whitsuntide days still lingers in the song of the chaffinch.

25

4. *Blackbirds*.

Let us imagine a perfect day near the end of February: a quiet day, the sun shining, the air mild; we get a few such days in every normal February. A lover of birds is walking in the bare woods, pleased with the various songs that he has already heard this year, listening especially to the loud song of dominant mistle-thrushes, fresh as the bright air, clear as the blue sky above; while little rills of robin song pour into his ears. Suddenly attention is arrested by something more rare in quality than the song of the mistle-thrush; he stops, listens, hears it again, and is assured of the authentic notes of a blackbird. . . . It is not possible to explain why the blackbird's notes excel and why they mean so much to us. To me there is something in it that I can best describe as intimacy. The songs of other birds please or delight us, but that of the blackbird seems to make a direct appeal to us and stirs some inward emotion. . . . The song is a linked phrase, repeated again and again at intervals. As a rule the bird chooses a perch for the purpose of singing, but occasionally changes its place and sings while flying from one perch to another. It is a supreme moment when a blackbird, passing from one bush of flowering hawthorn to another, as if one spot could not contain its joy, utters its song on the wing in the ecstasy of mid-May.

5. *Nightingales*.

Let us suppose a lover of birds' song to be walking, slowly, with ears alert, about an oak wood in the latter part of May. The big trees stand sufficiently apart to encourage plenty of undergrowth—thickets of thorn and of bramble, hazel, and perhaps some bushes of whin. He hears, one after another, various songs familiar to him—thrush, blackbird, garden-warbler, black-cap, willow-warbler, whitethroat, and others; he selects the song of each with pleased attention: suddenly he is struck—it is almost a physical impact—by notes of an energy, force and dominance with which none of the others can compare. The song is not a linked phrase, like that of the blackbird: it is repetition of one set of notes; then a pause, and then a different set of notes: in this the plan of the song resembles that of the thrush. We cannot tell which notes will follow a pause. " Jug-jug-jug " is an expression used to describe the most usual and typical notes. But the supreme achievement of the nightingale is a loud, clear, sustained note that fills the air. The best notes of other birds, blackbird or blackcap, for instance, come distinctly from the point where the bird utters them, and seem to reach and terminate at the listener's ear; but the supreme notes of the nightingale envelop and surround us: so that we lose perception of the point whence they proceed: it is as if we were included and embraced in pervading sound.

6. *Robins.*

Any male robin can be tamed; such at least is my experience. The bird is first attracted by crumbs of bread thrown on the ground; then a meal-worm is thrown to it; then a box—such as one of the small metal boxes in which chemists sell lozenges—is placed open on the ground with meal-worms in it. When the bird has become used to this, the next step is to kneel down and place the back of one hand flat upon the

27

ground with the box open on the upturned palm, and the fingers projecting beyond the box. This is the most difficult stage, but robins will risk their lives for meal-worms, and the bird will soon face the fingers and stand on them. The final stage, that of getting the bird to come on to the hand when raised above the ground, is easy. The whole process may be a matter of only two or three days in hard weather, when birds are hungry; and when once it has been accomplished the robin does not lose its tameness: confidence has been established and does not diminish when weather becomes mild and food plentiful.

Viscount Grey of Fallodon

XXVI: HUDSON AND HIS WIFE AFOOT

I am a walker still, but with other means of getting about I do not feel so native to the earth as formerly. That is a loss. Yet a poorer walker it would have been hard to find, and on even my most prolonged wanderings the end of each day usually brought extreme fatigue. This, too, although my only companion was slow—slower than the poor proverbial snail or tortoise —and I would leave her half a mile or so behind to force my way through unkept hedges, climb hills, and explore woods and thickets to converse with every bird and shy little beast and scaly creature I could discover. But mark what follows. In the late afternoon I would be back in the road or footpath, satisfied to go slow, then slower still, until the snail in woman shape would be obliged to slacken her pace to keep me company, and even to stand still at intervals to give me needful rest.

But there were compensations, and one, perhaps the best of all, was that this method of seeing the country made us more intimate with the people we met and stayed with. They were mostly poor people, cottagers in small remote villages: and we, too, were poor, often footsore, in need of their ministrations, and nearer to them on that account than if we had travelled in a more comfortable way. I can recall a hundred little adventures we met with during those wanderings, when we walked day after day, without map or guide-book as our custom was, not knowing where the evening would find us, but always confident that the people to whom it would fall in the end to shelter us would prove interesting to know and would show us a kindness that money could not pay for.

.   .   .   .   .

In walking, even in that poor way, when, on account of physical weakness, it was often a pain and weariness, there are alleviations which may be more to us than positive pleasures, and scenes to delight the eye that are missed by the wheelmen in his haste, or but dimly seen or vaguely surmised in passing—green refreshing nooks and crystal streamlets, and shadowy woodland depths with glimpses of a blue sky beyond—all in the wilderness of the human heart.

W. H. Hudson

XXVII: WHY DO YOU GO THE SAME ROAD
EVERY DAY?

A friend said: " Why do you go the same road
every day? Why not have a change and walk somewhere else sometimes? Why keep on up and down
the same place? " I could not answer; till then it had
not occurred to me that I did always go one way; as
for the reason of it I could not tell; I continued in my
old mind while the summers went away. Not till
years afterwards was I able to see why I went the
same round and did not care for change. I do not
want change; I want the same old and loved things,
the same wild-flowers, the same trees and soft ash-
green; the same turtle-doves, the blackbirds, the
coloured yellowhammer sing, sing, singing so long as
there is light to cast a shadow on the dial, for such is
the measure of his song, and I want them in the same
place. Let me find them morning after morning, the
starry-white petals radiating, striving upwards to
their ideal. Let me see the idle shadows resting on the
white dust; let me hear the humble-bees, and stay to
look down on the rich dandelion disk. Let me see the
very thistles opening their great crowns—I should
miss the thistles; the reed-grasses hiding the moor-
hen; the bryony bine, at first crudely ambitious and
lifted by force of youthful sap straight above the
hedgerow to sink of its own weight presently and progress with crafty tendrils; swifts shot through the air
with outstretched wings like crescent-headed shaftless
arrows darted from the clouds; the chaffinch with a
feather in her bill; all the living staircase of the spring,
step by step, upwards to the great gallery of the

summer—let me watch the same succession year by year.

Why, I knew the very dates of them all—the reddening elm, the arum, the hawthorn leaf, the celandine, the may; the yellow iris of the waters, the heath of the hillside. The time of the nightingale—the place to hear the first note; onwards to the drooping fern and the time of the redwing—the place of *his* first note, so welcome to the sportsman as the acorn ripens and the pheasant, come to the age of manhood, feeds himself; onwards to the shadowless days—the long shadowless winter, for in winter it is the shadows we miss as much as the light. They lie over the summer sward, design upon design, dark lace on green and gold; they glorify the sunlight: they repose on the distant hills like Gods upon Olympus; without shadow, what even is the sun? At the foot of the great cliffs by the sea you may know this, it is dry glare; mighty ocean is dearer as the shadows of the clouds sweep over as they sweep over the green corn. Past the shadowless winter, when it is all shade, and therefore no shadow; onwards to the first coltsfoot and on to the seed-time again; I knew the dates of all of them. I did not want change; I wanted the same flowers to return on the same day, the titlark to rise soaring from the same oak to fetch down love with a song from heaven to his mate on the nest beneath. No change, no new thing; if I found a fresh wild-flower in a fresh place, still it wove at once into the old garland. In vain, the very next year was different even in the same place—*that* had been a year of rain, and the flag flowers were wonderful to see; *this* was a dry year, and the flags not half the height, the gold of the flower not so deep; next year the fatal billhook came and

31

swept away a slow-grown hedge that had given me crab-blossom in cuckoo-time and hazelnuts in harvest. Never again the same, even in the same place.

A little feather droops downward to the ground—a swallow's feather fuller of miracle than the Pentateuch—how shall that feather be placed again ·in the breast where it grew? Nothing twice. Time changes the places that knew us, and if we go back in after years, still even then it is not the old spot; the gate swings differently, new thatch has been put on the old gables, the road has been widened, and the sward the driven sheep lingered on is gone. Who dares to think then? For faces fade as flowers, and there is no consolation. So now I am sure I was right in always walking the same way by the starry flowers striving upwards on a slender ancestry of stem; I would follow the plain old road to-day if I could. Let change be far from me; that irresistible change must come is bitter indeed. Give me the old road, the same flowers—they were only stitchwort—the old succession of days and garland, ever weaving into it fresh wild-flowers from far and near. Fetch them from distant mountains, discover them on decaying walls, in unsuspected corners; though never seen before, still they are the same: there has been a place in my heart waiting for them.

Richard Jefferies

XXVIII: THE JOYS OF THE ROAD

Now the joys of the road are chiefly these:
A crimson touch on the hard-wood trees

A vagrant's morning wide and blue,
In early fall, when the wind walks, too;

A shadowy highway cool and brown,
Alluring up and enticing down

From rippled water to dappled swamp,
From purple glory to scarlet pomp;

The outward eye, the quiet will,
And the striding heart from hill to hill;

The tempter apple over the fence;
The cobweb bloom on the yellow quince;

The palish asters along the wood—
A lyric touch of the solitude;

An open hand, an easy shoe,
And a hope to make the day go through—

Another to sleep with, and a third
To wake me up at the voice of a bird;

A scrap of gossip at the ferry;
A comrade neither glum nor merry,

Who never defers and never demands,
But, smiling, takes the world in his hands,—

Seeing it good as when God first saw
And gave it the weight of his will for law.

And O the joy that is never won,
But follows and follows the journeying sun,

By marsh and tide, by meadow and stream,
A will-o'-the-wind, a light-o'-dream,

The racy smell of the forest loam
When the stealthy, sad-heart leaves go home;

The broad gold wake of the afternoon;
The silent fleck of the cold new moon;

The sound of the hollow sea's release
From stormy tumult to starry peace;

With only another league to wend;
And two brown arms at the journey's end!

These are the joys of the open road—
For him who travels without a load.

Bliss Carman

XXIX: THE SANTA-FÉ TRAIL

This is the order of the music of the morning:—
First, from the far East comes but a crooning.
The crooning turns to a sunrise singing.
Hark to the *calm*-horn, *balm*-horn, *psalm*-horn.
Hark to the *faint*-horn, *quaint*-horn, *saint*-horn....

Hark to the *pace*-horn, *chase*-horn, *race*-horn.
And the holy veil of the dawn has gone.
Swiftly the brazen car comes on.
It burns in the East as the sunrise burns.
I see great flashes where the far trail turns.
Its eyes are lamps like the eyes of dragons.
It drinks gasoline from big red flagons.
Butting through the delicate mists of the morning,
It comes like lightning, goes past roaring.
It will hail all the windmills, taunting, ringing,
Dodge the cyclones,
Count the milestones,
On through the ranges the prairie-dog tills—
Scooting past the cattle on the thousand hills. . . .
Ho for the tear-horn, scare-horn, dare-horn,
Ho for the *gay*-horn, *bark*-horn, *bay*-horn.
Ho for Kansas, land that restores us
When houses choke us, and great books bore us!
Sunrise Kansas, harvesters' Kansas,
A million men have found you before us.

I want live things in their pride to remain.
I will not kill one grasshopper vain,
Though he eats a hole in my shirt like a door.
I let him out, give him one chance more.
Perhaps, while he gnaws my hat in his whim,
Grasshopper lyrics occur to him.

I am a tramp by the long trail's border,
Given to squalor, rags and disorder.
I nap and amble and yawn and look,
Write fool-thoughts in my grubby book,
Recite to the children, explore at my ease,
Work when I work, beg when I please,

35

Give crank-drawings, that make folks stare,
To the half-grown boys in the sunset glare,
And get me a place to sleep in the hay
At the end of a live-and-let-live day.

I find in the stubble of the new-cut weeds
A whisper and a feasting, all one needs:
The whisper of the strawberries, white and red
Here where the new-cut weeds lie dead.

But I would not walk all alone till I die
Without some life-drunk horns going by.
Up round this apple-earth they come
Blasting the whispers of the morning dumb:—
Cars in a plain realistic row.
And fair dreams fade
When the raw horns blow.

On each snapping pennant
A big black name:—
The careering city
Whence each car came.
They tour from Memphis, Atlanta, Savannah,
Tallahassee and Texarkana.
They tour from Peoria, Davenport, Kankakee.
Cars from Concord, Niagara, Boston,
Cars from Topeka, Emporia, and Austin.
Cars from Chicago, Hannibal, Cairo.
Cars from Alton, Oswego, Toledo.
Cars from Buffalo, Kokomo, Delphi,
Cars from Lodi, Carmi, Loami.
Ho for Kansas, land that restores us
When houses choke us, and great books bore us!
While I watch the highroad

And look at the sky,
While I watch the clouds in amazing grandeur
Roll their legions without rain
Over the blistering Kansas plain—
While I sit by the milestone
And watch the sky,
The United States
Goes by.

Listen to the iron-horns, ripping, racking,
Listen to the quack-horns, slack and clacking.
Way down the road, trilling like a toad,
Here comes the *dice*-horn, here comes the *vice*-horn,
Here comes the *snarl*-horn, *brawl*-horn, *lewd*-horn,
Followed by the *prude*-horn, bleak and squeaking:—
(Some of them from Kansas, some of them from Kan-
    sas.)
Here comes the *hod*-horn, *plod*-horn, *sod*-horn,
Nevermore-to-*roam*-horn, *loam*-horn, *home*-horn.
(Some of them from Kansas, some of them from Kan-
    sas.)
    Far away the Rachel-Jane
    Not defeated by the horns
    Sings amid a hedge of thorns:—
    " Love and life,
    Eternal youth—
    Sweet, sweet, sweet, sweet,
    Dew and glory,
    Love and truth,
    Sweet, sweet, sweet, sweet.
WHILE SMOKE-BLACK FREIGHTS ON THE DOUBLE-
    TRACKED RAILROAD,
DRIVEN AS THOUGH BY THE FOUL FIEND'S OX-GOAD,

SCREAMING TO THE WEST COAST, SCREAMING TO THE
  EAST,
CARRY OFF A HARVEST, BRING BACK A FEAST,
HARVESTING MACHINERY AND HARNESS FOR THE
  BEAST,
THE HAND-CARS WHIZ, AND RATTLE ON THE RAILS,
THE SUNLIGHT FLASHES ON THE TIN DINNER-PAILS.
And then, in an instant,
Ye modern men,
Behold the procession once again,
Listen to the iron-horns, ripping, racking,
Listen to the *wise*-born, desperate-to-*advise* horn,
Listen to the *fast*-horn, *kill*-horn, *blast*-horn. . . .

    Far away the Rachel-Jane
    Now defeated by the horns
    Sings amid a hedge of thorns:—
    Love and life,
    Eternal youth,
    Sweet, sweet, sweet, sweet,
    Dew and glory,
    Love and truth.
    Sweet, sweet, sweet, sweet.

The mufflers open on a score of cars
With wonderful thunder,
CRACK, CRACK, CRACK,
CRACK-CRACK, CRACK-CRACK,
CRACK, CRACK, CRACK,
Listen to the gold-horn
Old-horn. . . .
Cold-horn. . . .
And all of the tunes, till the night comes down
On hay-stack, and ant-hill, and wind-bitten town.
Then far in the west, as in the beginning,
Dim in the distance, sweet in retreating,

Hark to the faint-horn, quaint-horn, saint-horn,
Hark to the calm-horn, balm-horn, psalm-horn. . . .

They are hunting the goals that they understand:—
San-Francisco and the brown sea-sand.
My goal is the mystery the beggars win.
I am caught in the web that the night-winds spin.
The edge of the wheat-ridge speaks to me.
I talk with the leaves of the mulberry-tree.
And now I hear, as I sit all alone
In the dusk, by another big Santa-Fé stone,
The souls of the tall corn gathering round
And the gay little souls of the grass in the ground.
Listen to the tale that the cottonwood tells.
Listen to the windmills, singing o'er the wells.
Listen to the whistling flutes without price
Of myriad prophets out of Paradise.
Harken to the wonder
That the night-air carries. . . .
Listen . . . to . . . the . . . whisper . . .
Of . . . the . . . prairie . . . fairies
      Singing o'er the fairy plain:—
      " Sweet, sweet, sweet, sweet.
      Love and glory,
      Stars and rain,
      Sweet, sweet, sweet, sweet . . ."

Vachel Lindsay

XXX: THE OPEN SECRET

Sweet secret of the open air—
　　That waits so long, and always there, unheeded.
　　Something uncaught, so free, so calm large confi-
　　　　dent—
　　The floating breeze, the far hills and broad sky,
　　And every little bird and tiny fly or flower
　　At home in the great whole, nor feeling lost at all or
　　　　forsaken,
　　Save man—slight man!

　　He, Cain-like from the calm eyes of the Angels,
　　In houses hiding, in huge gas-lighted offices and
　　　　dens, in ponderous churches,
　　Beset with darkness, cowers;
　　And like some hunted criminal torments his brain
　　For fresh means of escape, continually;
　　Builds thicker higher walls, ramparts of stone and
　　　　gold, piles flesh and skins of slaughtered beasts,
　　'Twixt him and that he fears;
　　Fevers himself with plans, works harder and harder,
　　And wanders far and farther from the goal.

　　And still the great World waits by the door as ever,
　　The great World stretching endlessly on every hand,
　　　　in deep on deep of fathomless content—
　　Where sing the Morning stars in joy together,
　　And all things are at home.

Edward Carpenter

XXXI: THE ROAD TO HIRSCHAU

P<small>RINCE</small> H<small>ENRY</small> and E<small>LSIE</small>, with their attendants

> *Elsie.* Onward and onward the
> highway runs to the distant
> city, impatiently bearing
> Tidings of human joy and disaster,
> of love and of hate, of doing
> and daring!
> *Prince Henry.* This life of ours
> is a wild aeolian harp of many
> a joyous strain,
> But under them all there runs a
> loud perpetual wail, as of souls
> in pain.
> *Elsie.* Faith alone can interpret
> life, and the heart that aches
> and bleeds with the stigma
> Of pain, alone bears the likeness of
> Christ, and can comprehend
> its dark enigma.
> *Prince Henry.* Man is selfish,
> and seeketh pleasure with little
> care of what may betide;
> Else why am I travelling here
> beside thee, a demon that
> rides by an angel's side?
> *Elsie.* All the hedges are white
> with dust, and the great dog
> under the creaking wain,
> Hangs his head in the lazy heat
> while onward the horses toil
> and strain.

41

Prince Henry. Now they stop
  at the wayside inn, and the
  wagoner laughs with the land-
  lord's daughter,
While out of the dripping trough
  the horses distend their
  leathern sides with water.
Elsie. All through life there are
  wayside inns, where man may
  refresh his soul with love;
Even the lowest may quench his
  thirst at rivulets fed by springs
  from above.
Prince Henry. Yonder, where
  rises the cross of stone, our
  journey along the highway
  ends,
And over the fields, by a bridle
  path, down into the broad
  green valley descends.
Elsie. I am not sorry to leave
  behind the beaten road with
  its dust and heat;
The air will be sweeter far, and the
  turf will be softer under our
  horses' feet.
  (*They turn down a green lane.*)

Henry Wadsworth Longfellow

XXXII: AUGURIES OF INNOCENCE

To see a world in a grain of sand,
  And a heaven in a wild flower;
Hold infinity in the palm of your hand,
  And eternity in an hour.

A Robin Redbreast in a cage
Puts all heaven in a rage;
A dove-house filled with doves and pigeons
Shudders hell through all its regions.
A dog starved at his master's gate
Predicts the ruin of the state;
A game-cock clipped and armed for fight
Doth the rising sun affright;
A horse misused upon the road
Calls to Heaven for human blood.
Every wolf and lion's howl
Raises from hell a human soul;
Each outcry of the hunted hare
A fibre from the brain doth tear;
A skylark wounded on the wing
Doth make a cherub cease to sing.
He who shall hurt the little wren
Shall never be beloved by men;
He who the ox to wrath has moved
Shall never be by woman loved;
He who shall train the horse to war
Shall never pass the Polar Bar.
The wanton boy that kills the fly
Shall feel the spider's enmity;
He who torments the chafer's sprite
Weaves a bower in endless night.

The caterpillar on the leaf
Repeats to thee thy mother's grief;
The wild deer wandering here and there
Keep the human soul from care:
The lamb misused breeds public strife,
And yet forgives the butcher's knife.
Kill not the moth nor butterfly,
For the last judgment draweth nigh;
The beggar's dog and widow's cat,
Feed them and thou shalt grow fat.
Every tear from every eye
Becomes a babe in eternity;
The bleat, the bark, bellow and roar,
Are waves that beat on Heaven's shore.
The bat that flits at close of eve
Has left the brain that won't believe;
The owl that calls upon the night
Speaks the unbeliever's fright.
The gnat that sings his summer's song
Poison gets from Slander's tongue;
The poison of the snake and newt
Is the sweat of Envy's foot;
The poison of the honey bee
Is the artist's jealousy;
The strongest poison ever known
Came from Cæsar's laurel crown.

.   .   .   .   .

He who mocks the infant's faith
Shall be mocked in age and death;
He who shall teach the child to doubt
The rotten grave shall ne'er get out;
He who respects the infant's faith
Triumphs over hell and death.

The babe is more than swaddling bands
Throughout all these human lands;
Tools were made, and born were hands,
Every farmer understands.
The questioner who sits so sly
Shall never know how to reply.
He who replies to words of doubt
Doth put the light of knowledge out;
A puddle, or the cricket's cry,
Is to doubt a fit reply.
The child's toys and the old man's reasons
Are the fruit of the two seasons.
The emmet's inch and eagle's mile
Make lame philosophy to smile.
A truth that's told with bad intent
Beats all the lies you can invent.
He who doubts from what he sees
Will ne'er believe, do what you please;
If the sun and moon should doubt
They'd immediately go out.

Every night and every morn
Some to misery are born;
Every morn and every night
Some are born to sweet delight;
Some are born to sweet delight,
Some are born to endless night.
Joy and woe are woven fine,
A clothing for the soul divine;
Under every grief and pine
Runs a joy with silken twine—
It is right it should be so;
Man was made for joy and woe;

And, when this we rightly know
Safely through the world we go.
We are led to believe a lie
When we see *with* not *through* the eye,
Which was born in a night to perish in a night
When the soul slept in beams of light.
God appears and God is light
To those poor souls who dwell in night:
But doth a human form display
To those who dwell in realms of day.

William Blake

XXXIII: THE PIED PIPER LEADS THE CHILDREN AWAY

Once more he stept into the street
And to his lips again
Laid his long pipe of smooth straight cane;
And ere he blew three notes (such sweet
Soft notes as yet musician's cunning
Never gave the enraptured air)
There was a rustling that seemed like a bustling
Of merry crowds justling at pitching and hustling,
Small feet were pattering, wooden shoes clattering,
Little hands clapping and little tongues chattering,
And, like fowls in a farmyard when barley is scat-
      tering,
Out came the children running.
All the little boys and girls,
With rosy cheeks and flaxen curls,
And sparkling eyes and teeth like pearls,
Tripping and skipping, ran merrily after
The wonderful music with shouting and laughter.

The mayor was dumb, and the Council stood
As if they were changed into blocks of wood,
Unable to move a step, or cry
To the children merrily skipping by,
—Could only follow with the eye
The joyous crowd at the Piper's back.
But how the Mayor was on the rack,
And the wretched Council's bosoms beat,
As the Piper turned from the High Street
To where the Weser rolled its waters

Right in the way of their sons and daughters!
However he turned from South to West,
And to Koppelberg Hill his steps addressed,
And after him the children pressed;
Great was the joy in every breast.
" He never can cross that mighty top!
He's forced to let the piping drop,
And we shall see our children stop! "
When lo, as they reached the mountain-side,
A wondrous portal opened wide,
As if a cavern was suddenly hollowed,
And the Piper advanced and the children followed;
And when all were in to the very last,
The door in the mountain-side shut fast.
Did I say all? No! One was lame,
And could not dance the whole of the way;
And in after years, if you would blame
His sadness, he was used to say—
" It's dull in our town since my playmates left!
I can't forget that I'm bereft
Of all the pleasant sights they see,
Which the Piper also promised me.
For he led us, he said, to a joyous land,
Joining the town and just at hand,
Where waters gushed and fruit-trees grew
And flowers put forth a fairer hue,
And everything was strange and new;
The sparrows were brighter than peacocks here,
And their dogs outran our fallow deer,
And horses were born with eagles' wings,
And honey-bees had lost their stings.
And just as I became assured
My lame foot would be speedily cured,
The music stopped and I stood still,

49   E

And found myself outside the hill.
Left alone against my will,
To go now limping as before,
And never hear of that country more! "

Robert Browning

XXXIV: THE LOST PIBROCH

" I did not tell you that the Lost *Piobaireachd* is the
piobaireachd of good-byes. It is the tune of broken
clans that sets the men on the foray and makes cold
hearth-stones. It was played in Glenshira when
Gilleasbuig Gruamach could stretch stout swordsmen
from Boshang to Ben Bhuidhe, and where are the
folks of Glenshira this day? I saw a cheery night in
Carnus that's over Lochow, and song and story busy
about the fire, and the Moideart man played it for
a wager. In the morning the weans were without
fathers and Carnus men were scattered about the
wide world."

" It must be the magic tune, sure enough," said
Gilian.

" Magic, indeed, *laochain!* It is the tune that puts
men on the open road, that makes restless lads and
seeking women. Here's a Half Town of dreamers and
men fattening for want of men's work. They forget
the world is wide and round about their fir-trees, and
I can make them crave for something they cannot
name."

. . . He put up his pipe again, filled the bag at a
breath, brought the booming to the drones, and then
the chanter-reed cried sharp and high.

. . . The groundwork of the tune was a drumming

on the deep notes where the sorrows lie—" Come, come, come, my children, rain on the brae and the wind blowing."

" It is a salute," said Rory.

" It's the strange tune anyway," said Gilian ; "listen to the time of yon! "

The tune searched through Half Town and into the gloomy pinewood ; it put an end to the whoop of the night-hag and rang to Ben Bhreac. Boatmen deep and far on the loch could hear it, and Half Town folks sat up to listen.

Its story was the story that's ill to tell—something of the heart's longing and the curious chances of life. It bound up all the tales of all the clans, and made one tale of the Gael's past. Dirk nor sword against the tartan, but the tartan against all else, and the Gael's target fending the hill-land and the juicy straths from the pock-pitted little black men. The winters and the summers passing fast and furious, day and night roaring in the ears, and then again the clans at variance, and warders on every pass and on every parish.

Then the tune changed.

" Folks," said the reeds, coaxing. " Wide's the world and merry the road. Here's but the old story and the women we kissed before. Come, come to the flat-lands rich and full, where the wonderful new things happen and the women's lips are still to try! "

" To-morrow," said Gilian in his friend's ear— " to-morrow I will go jaunting to the North. It has been in my mind since Beltae."

" One might be doing worse," said Rory, " and I have the notion to try a trip with my cousin to the foreign wars."

The blind piper put up his shoulder higher and

51

rolled the air into the *crunluadh breabach* that comes prancing with variations. Pride stiffened him from heel to hip, and hip to head, and set his sinews like steel.

He was telling of the gold to get for the searching, and the bucks that may be had for the hunting. "What," said the reeds, "are your poor crops, slashed by the constant rain and rotting, all for a scart in the bottom of a pot? What are your stots and heifers—black, dun, and yellow—to milch-cows and horses? Here's but the same for ever—toil and sleep, sleep and toil ever on, no feud nor foray nor castles to harry —only the starved field and the sleeping moss. Let us to a brisker place! Over yonder are the long straths and the deep rivers and townships strewn thick as your corn-rigs; over yonder's the place of the pack-men's tales and the packmen's wares: steep we the withies and go!"

The two men stood with heads full of bravery and dreaming-men in a carouse. "This," said they, "is the notion we had, but had no words for. It's a poor trade piping and eating and making amusement when one might be wandering up and down the world. We must be packing the haversacks."

Then the *crunluadh mach* came fast and furious on the chanter, and Half Town shook with it. It buzzed in the ear like the flowers in the Honey Croft, and made commotion among the birds rocking on their eggs in the wood.

"*So! so!*" barked the *iolair* on Craig-an-eas. "I have heard before it was an ill thing to be satisfied; in the morning I'll try the kids on Maam-side, for the hares here are wersh and tough." "Hearken, dear," said the *londubh*. "I know now why my beak is gold;

it is because I once ate richer berries than the whortle, and in season I'll look for them on the braes of Glenfinne." " Honk-unk," said the fox, the cunning red fellow, " am not I the fool to be staying on this little brae when I know so many roads elsewhere? "

And the people sitting up in their beds in Half Town moaned for something new. " Paruig Dall is putting the strange tune on her there," said they. " What the meaning of it is we must ask in the morning, but, *ochanoch!* it leaves one hungry at the heart." And then gusty winds came snell from the north, and where the dark crept first, the day made his first showing, so that Ben Ime rose black against a grey sky.

" That's the Lost *Piobaireachd*," said Paruig Dall when the bag sank on his arm.

Neil Munro

XXXV: THE SCOTS GUARDS ENTER GERMANY

In all these wanderings the pipers were our companions, leading us and exploring the way. Two days, indeed, our instrumental band shared the honours with the pipers and we took our step to the solemn chanting march of " Sambre et Meuse," but the General intervened. We must not march to instrumental music and this band must cease. So before and after this instrumental blare of brass it was the slogan alone that we followed.

The various companies of the battalion took it in turn to be first in the march, to be second, to be third, to follow up the rear, and when the company was in front it heard the music in all its immediacy and splendour, but when it was behind it only heard it far away like a child's voice sobbing or calling now and then. Passing over the crest of a hill the music rose with the height and then became silent as the vanguard dipped into the hollow beyond, rising however again from the basin of the valley and resounding back in increasing volume and happiness. When the road turned half-right skirting a hill, the whole rearguard was enlivened by the pipes coming as it were toward them. When the road lay even over marshes and plains the music was deadened, but when we entered forests bits sprang to life as if the woodland were full of pipers—a clamorous, exulting, echoing music, that of the woods! And in the gorges and ravines Nature responded also from the rocks.

Wonderful pipes! The men are inclined to grumble and fall out, but the pipes make a unity of them. Invisible tendons and muscles seem to connect the legs of all files, and all move as one, mechanically, rhythmically, certainly. The strong are reduced to the step, the weak are braced up to it. All bear the strain and share the strain. So we go on, and the miracle is in the power of the music.

The first weeks of our journeying were punctuated by long halts, but the last ten days in the wettest of the weather were continuous marches. They made the most trying time of our experience. Boots wore out. Clothes got wet through and could not be dried. Rations were often delayed, and from continuous wearing of our heavy packs our shoulders were galled. But the curiosity to see Germany, the sense of an adventure, and the music, kept our spirits up. At each new turn of the road the evenly-pacing Highlanders in the vanguard of our column felt the way, explored the new way, playing as they went.

Thus on the morning of the 12th December, parading in the wet before dawn, all in our waterproof capes, we left the last forlorn village of the Belgian Ardennes and climbed out to the mysterious line which we all wished to see, that put friendly land behind and left only enemy country in front. One asked oneself what Germany would be like. But only an hour was needed to bring us to the custom-houses and the sentry-posts. We marched to attention, the rain streamed off our capes and trickled from our hats, but the tireless pipers played ahead, and by someone's inspiration the word went to the pipe-major, play " Over the Border "; so with a skirl that no weather could suppress we came up to the line to the strains of

> March, march, all in good order,
> All the blue bonnets are over the Border.

Then the pipers separated from the main body and took up their stand in a phalanx by the side of the road beside the familiar figure of our Brigadier, and they played " Hieland Laddie " whilst we marched past at the salute. Thus we entered Germany with no formalities and no enemy in view. We felt much cheered though the time was cheerless, and we were full of curiosity to see the people we still called Huns, and men still talked of bayoneting and cutting throats. Presently we began to pass cottages, and we stared at them, but could see no people. Some of us shouted: " Come out and show yourselves " and " Come out of hiding," forgetting that " Jerry," as we called him, was hardly likely to be awake properly yet.

When we began to see Germans they paid no attention to us whatever, but the woman at the well went on drawing water and the man with straw in his arms continued his way to his barn without vouchsafing a glance. We saw women talking with their backs to us, and they did not turn round to look at us as we passed. The children were as nonchalant towards the gay figures of our kilties as if they saw pipers every day of the week. It must be said we were a little taken aback, a little mortified. But it rained and rained and the drums became silent, sodden and soaked with the water, and we splashed patiently and mechanically on through the mud and over the broken roads. Our fours became twos, became long threads of single file as we picked our way amidst great holes and ruts and gliding rivers of yellow ooze. When there would otherwise have been a view of Germany, trailing mist, liquefying in the wind to bitter rain, swept hither and thither across our faces. On the sides of the roads was desolation, and occasionally still, as in Belgium, the sinister grey heaps of the entrails of cows which told of the indisciplined German Army which had retired before us.

And with everyone wet to the bone we climbed the excruciatingly broken road over the hill from Amel to Moderscheide. In this wretched German village we were billeted, and the men made huge bonfires in the barnyards, and stood round them to dry themselves. The Germans seemed to be rather afraid of us, and servile, but very poor. Tottering old men insisted on shaking hands with us. The girls of the place seemed to be carefully kept out of our way. Billets were wretched, and the men, still fire-eating, hunted for better ones which, when they found, they intended to take by storm. Those who had revolvers expected to have to use them. But we only discovered that the native inhabitants slept in worse places than we had, and that everyone was of the mildest disposition. Our blankets and reserve rations were in the wagons stuck at the bottom of the Amel hill. There was only one thing to do—to get dry and make the best of it.

Next day, with the skies still streaming, we made the longest continuous march, some thirty-six kilometres, and by that effort we got well into Germany. The roads improved as we got further on, but the tramp through the forest of Zitter was long, marshy, and melancholy. Our company was first after the pipers, and had the full benefit of the music all the way. And we wandered inward, inward, with our seeking and haunting Gaelic melodies, into the depths of the hanging silent wood. It was strange how aloof Nature seemed to these melodies. In Scotland, or even in France, all the hills and the woods would have helped the music. But in this German land all were cold toward us, and those endless pine-trees seemed to be holding hands with fingers spread before the eyes to show their shame and humiliation. There was a curious sense that the road on which we trod was not our road, and that earth and her fruits on either hand were hostile.

And how tired the men became, with half of them through the soles of their boots and with racking damp in their shoulders and backs from their rain-sodden packs! But we listened still, whilst voluminous waves of melody wandered homeless over German wastes and returned to us:

I heard the pibroch sounding, sounding,
    O'er the wide meadows and lands from afar,
or to the stirring strains of the " March of the Battle
of Harlaw " or to the crooning, hoping, sobbing of
" Lord Lovat's Lament," and so went on from hour
to hour through the emptiness of southern Germany.
I thought of the wonderful theme which this march
offered to the musician, and knew in anticipation that
some day the world would possess some great musical
composition on the March to the Rhine—an " 1812 "
for Western Europe which some Tchaikovsky would
compose. I thought of its nature. Would it not begin
with the blare of brass obscuring the tremulous hopes
and fears of March 21, 1918? It would be noisy and
ambitious and terrifying and vulgar. But this vul-
garity would fail, met by the will of Britain, France,
America, Italy, Serbia, the will of the rest of humanity.
The fears would gain ground till the point of surrender
arrived. Then would commence the music of our
strange march. No, not one in which " Deutschland
über Alles " faded into " Rule Britannia " and the
" Marseillaise," not one of exultancy of victor and
utter rout of fleeting foe. But it would be sad, pene-
trating music, questing music, haunting music, all
subdued and, as it were, prostrated. The voices of the
German dead would rise into it, not exultantly, but
in curious sadness, as if they were unreconciled with
their own sacrifice; the German land and the German
forests would speak their shame in it, the German
gods would grow small and abase themselves, and all
that the proud Wagner ever conceived would die away
to a piping of birds in one note over wildernesses. The
fall of Germany was a greater event than the victory
of those who strove against her.

The pipes seemed to express the thought, the Gaelic wailing in the rain and the steady march through the ancient woods.

Still we swung along the way to the Rhine, and knew our halt could not be far. However, when we thought we had just about reached our camping-ground for the night, we came to a guide-post which showed it still to be seven kilometres on. But that was at the top of a long hill, and the road ran gently down through woods the whole way. The Colonel sent a message to play the light-hearted song of the " Men of Portree." The rain had stopped, and an evening sky unveiled a more cheerful light. So with an easy, inconsequent air we cast off care and tripped away down to the substantial and once prosperous bit of Rhineland called Hellenthal, well on our way to Cologne.   *Stephen Graham*

XXXVI: THE SONG OF THE BANJO

You couldn't pack a Broadwood half a mile—
    You mustn't leave a fiddle in the damp—
You couldn't raft an organ up the Nile,
    And play it in an Equatorial swamp.
I travel with the cooking-pots and pails—
    I'm sandwiched 'tween the coffee and the pork—
And when the dusty column checks and tails,
    You should hear me spur the rearguard to a walk!

With my " *Pilly-willy-winky-winky-popp!* "
    (Oh, it's any tune that comes into my head!)
So I keep 'em moving forward till they drop;
    So I play 'em up to water and to bed.

In the silence of the camp before the fight,
    When it's good to make your will and say your
        prayer,
You can hear my *strumpty-tumpty* overnight
    Explaining ten to one was always fair.
I'm the prophet of the Utterly Absurd,
    Of the Patently Impossible and Vain—
And when the Thing that Couldn't has occurred,
    Give me time to change my leg and go again.

        With my "*Tumpa-tumpa-tumpa-tum-pa tump!*"
            In the desert where the dung-fed camp-smoke
                curled
        There was never voice before us till I led our
            lonely chorus,
            I—the war-drum of the White Man round the
                world!

By the bitter road the Younger Son must tread,
    Ere he win to hearth and saddle of his own,—
'Mid the riot of the shearers at the shed,
    In the silence of the herder's hut alone—
In the twilight, on a bucket upside down,
    Hear me babble what the weakest won't confess—
I am Memory and Torment—I am Town!
    I am all that ever went with evening dress!

        With my " *Tunk-a tunka-tunka-tunka-tunk!*"
            (So the lights—the London lights—grow near
                and plain)
        So I rowel 'em afresh towards the Devil and the
            Flesh,
            Till I bring my broken rankers home again.

In desire of many marvels over sea,
　　Where the new-raised tropic city sweats and roars,
I have sailed with Young Ulysses from the quay
　　Till the anchor rumbled down on stranger shores.
He is blooded to the open and the sky,
　　He is taken in a snare that shall not fail,
He shall hear me singing strongly, till he die,
　　Like the shouting of a backstay in a gale.

　　With my " *Hya! Heeya! Heeya! Hullah! Haul!* "
　　　　(O the green that thunders aft along the deck!)
　　Are you sick o' towns and men? You must sign
　　　　and sail again,
　　　　For it's " Johnny Bowlegs, pack your kit and
　　　　trek! "

Through the gorge that gives the stars at noonday
　　clear—
　　Up the pass that packs the scud beneath our wheel—
Round the bluff that sinks her thousand fathom sheer—
　　Down the valley with our guttering brakes asqueal:
Where the trestle groans and quivers in the snow,
　　Where the many-shedded levels loop and twine,
So I lead my reckless children from below
　　Till we sing the Song of Roland to the pine.

　　With my " *Tinka-tinka-tinka-tinka-tink!* "
　　　　(And the axe has cleared the mountain, croup
　　　　and crest!)
　　So we ride the iron stallions down to drink,
　　　　Through the cañons to the waters of the West!

And the tunes that mean so much to you alone—
　　Common tunes that make you choke and blow your
　　nose,

Vulgar tunes that bring the laugh that brings the
    groan—
    I can rip your very heart-strings out with those;
With the feasting, and the folly, and the fun—
    And the lying, and the lusting, and the drink,
And the merry play that drops you, when you're done,
    To the thoughts that burn like irons if you think.

        With my " *Plunka-lunka-lunka-lunka-lunk!* "
            Here's a trifle on account of pleasure past,
        Ere the wit that made you win gives you eyes to
            see your sin
            And the heavier repentance at the last!

Let the organ moan her sorrow to the roof—
    I have told the naked stars the Grief of Man!
Let the trumpets snare the foeman to the proof—
    I have known Defeat, and mocked it as we ran!
My bray ye may not alter nor mistake
    When I stand to jeer the fatted Soul of Things,
But the Song of Lost Endeavour that I make,
    Is it hidden in the twanging of the strings?

        With my " *Ta-ra-rara-rara-ra-ra-rrrp!* "
            (Is it naught to you that hear and pass me by?
        But the word—the word is mine, when the order
            moves the line
            And the lean, locked ranks go roaring down to
            die.

The grandam of my grandam was the Lyre—
    (O the blue below the little fisher huts!)
That the Stealer stooping beachward filled with fire,
    Till she bore my iron head and ringing guts!

By the wisdom of the centuries I speak—
  To the tune of yestermorn I set the truth—
I, the joy of life unquestioned—I, the Greek—
  I, the everlasting Wonder Song of Youth!

  With my " *Tinka-tinka-tinka-tinka-tink!* "
    (What d'ye lack, my noble masters? What d'ye
      lack?)
  So I draw the world together link by link:
    Yea, from Delos up to Limerick and back!

Rudyard Kipling

XXXVII: WANDER-THIRST

Beyond the East the Sunrise; beyond the West the
  sea;
And East and West the Wander-Thirst that will not
  let me be;
It works in me like madness to bid me say good-bye,
For the seas call, and the stars call, and oh! the call
  of the sky!

I know not where the white road runs, nor what the
  blue hills are,
But a man can have the sun for friend, and for his
  guide a star;
And there's no end of voyaging when once the voice
  is heard,
For the rivers call, and the road calls, and oh! the
  call of a bird!

Yonder the long horizon lies, and there by night and
   day
The old ships draw to home again, the young ships
   sail away;
And come I may, but go I must, and if men ask you
   why,
You may put the blame on the stars and the sun, and
   the white road and the sky.

Gerald Gould

XXXVIII: A DREAM

" I will arise and go now, and go to Innisfree,
   And a small cabin build there, of clay and wattles
      made;
Nine bean rows will I have there, a hive for the
      honey-bee,
   And live alone in the bee-loud glade."

I had a dream; and in my dream I dreamed that the
haunting magic of those lines held in it a test by which
life was to be proved. It brought the spirit of the Celt
to bear upon our gross Saxon conventionalism. It
broke in upon our dull assemblies with the challenge
of an Eternal Pilgrimage. So I dreamed that I was
meant to carry the music of the poem with me where-
ever I went: and, just as Shelley startled the stagnant
coach-load by his sudden and earnest invitation to
the stout lady at his side:

" For God's sake, let us sit upon the ground,
   And tell sad stories of the death of kings; "

so I was suddenly to bring this test to bear upon any
meeting, or drawing-room party, or conference, or

gathering, in which I might find myself, and was to whisper abruptly in the midst:

" I will arise and go now: and go to Innisfree."

As I uttered it, a new atmosphere would swiftly come over the scene; a new perspective would be felt. It would be seen, at once, how far the particular occasion, on which the test was used, would be able to respond with a congenial reaction, or how far it would stand condemned by its hopeless impotence to meet the challenge. I seemed, in my dream, to be looking in, through door and window, at the people gathered for some reason inside, and watching their behaviour as they lifted their heads from dreary occupations or turned round from listening to interminable speeches, and caught, with startled ears, the whisper creeping round—

" I will arise and go now, and go to Innisfree:
    And live alone in the bee-loud glade."

Will they recognise the call? Will they become aware of the far horizons, and of the brooding peace, where the lake water laps with low sounds upon the shore? Will their stolid business, which had seemed to them to absorb the attention of the entire universe by its enormous bulk, suddenly shrink before their eyes into a very little thing? Will they hurry, and their haste after gold and honour shrivel up into contemptible futility, as they recall the nine bean-rows, and the one hive for the honey-bee? Will all the noise of a tumultuous commerce become as nothing, and die away out of their ears, to leave only the memory of the linnet's wings a-flutter in the live evening? Will the big world drop away from them for one blessed moment, as once again they remember how peace comes dropping slow from the veils of the morning? Or will they repudiate, with Anglo-Saxon indignation the silly interruption of the Celt? Will they send a beadle at once to clear the court? Will they gather up their foolish old hearts into a yet stiffer and stupider solemnity, as they turn themselves again, from this frivolous interruption, to the ridiculous business in which they were engaged? So the judgment will work itself out; and we shall all know what we are made of.

How good it would be, now and again, if the chairman of a stuffy committee—which had been getting crosser and crosser every minute, as it passed on through item after item of an endless agenda paper, and tempers were fretful, and six rival amendments had all got tangled up in one another, and it began to look as if they would sit there till Domesday—were to rise, and, in a quiet voice, to announce:

" I will arise and go now, and go to Innisfree,
    And a small cabin build there, of clay and wattles
        made."

It would give just that wholesome relief, that wider outlook, which were so sorely needed. All the amendments would drop at once to the ground, and we should rush out into the open air, and whoop for joy. It would not matter to us in the least what we had, or had not, carried. We should feel that there was only one thing that mattered—and that was to have

" Nine bean rows . . . and a hive for the honey-bee."

Or it might be a Mansion House meeting, and the Lord Mayor of London would just have invited the

66

Venerable the Archdeacon of Timbuktu to address the dull leaden-eyed rows of torpid ladies who are the despair of all orators; and then, just while the Archdeacon was clearing his throat, and before he was off on his first period, a thin sound like a gnat's song would thrill piercingly round, and every soul in the room would hear it said:

"' I will arise and go now, and go to Innisfree.''

And, in a moment, Mayor and Mansion House and Archdeacon would have vanished to Timbuktu, and we should only hear the bees in the glade, and see the beans in their nine rows, instead of those melancholy rows of stuffy velvet charis. . . .

It might even be possible to find an opportunity at some comfortable Mattins at eleven in the great West, while the congregation sit there with a stolid " Dearly Beloved " look in their cold faces, solid and plump in cushioned pomp, to let the low, quiet voice steal round from pew to pew, murmuring, as the heavy sermon drones on its dismal length, " Why do I sit here? Why am I not far, far away? Will this never end? I shall die if it goes on any longer. I have an idea: I will arise and go now, and go to Innisfree."

Ah! and what of those tired bored ladies in Hyde Park, driven by relentless fate round and round the terrible circuit, with cards to drop on their way home; and always cards, and calls, and calls, and cards? What if, to them, the deliverance came, and a new hope dawned, and each said to the other—

" I will arise and go now, and go to Innisfree,
    And a small cabin build there, of clay and wattles
        made "?

If we could, now and again, stop a middle-aged gentleman in Piccadilly, on his way to his club to sit in the bow window and grumble and swear at the world he sees through it, and softly, cunningly whisper our secret " I will arise "; would the old boy's blurred heart not stir, and his liver forget its congestion, and his toes shake off their gout: and would not those big leather chairs look ridiculous to him, and all the flunkies silly; and would he not know what life was meant for, and what an old ass he had been to make such a mess of it?

All healthy life responds to this challenge. By rising to it, it refuses to become the slave of its own handiwork. It is ever being tempted to imprison itself inside this vast civilisation which it has piled up for itself. . . . It is from this stupid and treacherous betrayal of its own lordship that the cry of the Celt recalls it. " This civilisation is your own," it cries, " therefore, you are bigger than it can ever be. Your life overlaps it. Your spirit passes out behind it. You can drop it all behind you: you can shed it off like an old garment. You can forget it. Your way of escape is always open. You can laugh at it; you can see what a poor thing it is; you are its maker, and it is but a troublesome toy after all. Break it up, if you are bored with it. Get up, and go far away from all this money-grubbing business which those burly Saxons are taking so seriously. It is all a bad joke. There is a whole world outside it, far better and sweeter. Come along! Don't sit there, plodding and doddering all day! Why not come with us?

" I will arise and go now, and go to Innisfree."

. . . What a relief . . . When all else comes to an end,

and society crumbles to pieces under the Socialistic aggressions of West Ham, there will still be lake water lapping on a low shore, and the evening will yet be alive with linnet's wings.

Henry Scott Holland

XXXIX

A man may desire to go to Mecca. His conscience tells him that he ought to go to Mecca. He fares forth, either by the aid of Cook's, or unassisted; he may probably never reach Mecca; he may drown before he gets to Port Said; he may perish ingloriously on the coast of the Red Sea; his desire may remain eternally frustrate. Unfulfilled aspiration may always trouble him. But he will not be tormented in the same way as the man who, desiring to reach Mecca, and harried by the desire to reach Mecca, never leaves Brixton.

It is something to have left Brixton. Most of us have not left Brixton. We have not even taken a cab to Ludgate Circus. . . . *Arnold Bennett*

XL

No philosopher has ever had a clearer conception of the true end of man than I had at the age of twelve. All forms of self-realisation were false save one; and that was, to get oneself cast away, by hook or by crook, upon a Desolate Island. Nothing else would satisfy. Let others go to Heaven if they would; let others be good or great; but let me be cast on some lonely palm-strewn shore in the uttermost parts of the earth.

L. P. Jacks

XLI

He must go, go, go away from here!
 On the other side the world he's overdue.
'Send your road is clear before you
When the old spring fret comes o'er you
And the Red Gods call for you!
                                    Rudyard Kipling

XLII

Is it not better, then, to be alone,
And love Earth only for its earthly sake?
By the blue rushing of the arrowy Rhone,
Or the pure bosom of its nursing lake,
Which feeds it as a mother who doth make
A fair but froward infant her own care,
Kissing its cries away as these awake—
Is it not better thus our lives to wear,
Than join the crushing crowd, doom'd to inflict
    or bear?

I live not in myself, but I become
Portion of that around me; and to me
High mountains are a feeling, but the hum
Of human cities torture: I can see
Nothing to loathe in nature, save to be
A link reluctant in a fleshly chain,
Class'd among creatures, when the soul can flee,
And with the sky, the peak, the heaving plain
Of ocean, or the stars, mingle, and not in vain.
                                    Byron

XLIII: THE BAND AT OAXACA, SOUTHERN MEXICO

The scene in the plaza at nightfall, when the whole population comes out in parade, is in its way a ballet, unrehearsed and yet faultless. The life of the whole seems to be the band up in the fine stand in the central circle of the square. There stands the perfect little Zapotec conductor facing another Indian, who, with gourds in his hands, waves his rattle with long arms; and on each side of them and around them is resounding brass. A fine discipline has been achieved and a military precision in play. German and Spanish compositions alternate. Marches and Spanish dances seem to have a preference, and with joyous clamour and seductive melodies take possession of every man, woman and child in the plaza. Most remarkable are the tatterdemalion crowds of Indians, who, in cotton slops and bits of old blankets tied together, tramp into town and creep out of the dirt and the dust to the inner court of the bandstand. There they crouch and stare, though they get the music in ear-breaking blasts, being far too close. But they love to hear in the midst of it the rattle of the gourd players, the rattle of the raindrops as in their own half-forgotten rituals. Huddled together they stare at the brass, at the gourds, at the Zapotec bandmaster in his perfectly ironed regimentals.

From the inner court of the bandstand go six shady tracks, under palms and scarlet-flowering trees, and orange fruits dripping from boughs, and pomegranate trees; and these tracks reach the broad inner court, round which like mystic shapes the great crowd comes and goes.

Here run the newsboys crying, "Patria, Patria," and boys with dozens of bottles on their little heads shouting, "Frescos, frescos," and scores of boot-blacks with little wooden stools calling to all and sundry, "Grasar, grasar." Here walk stately ice-cream merchants with coloured barrels balanced on their heads, and swarthy sunburned men with sheaves of blankets for sale. Every Indian wears a blanket either slit at the middle for his head to go through or swathed about his body from head to foot as the Arab wears his burnous. Scarlet and orange are the com-monest colours of these blankets. They wear their sombreros, the poor ones of straw, the rich ones of felt, Popocatepetls of felt, high-domed, vastly brimmed embroidered. Here are grey hats all decorated with sailing ships and anchors worked in brown silk. Here are white hats bedizened with silver tinsel sewn on as the Indian women sew beetle-backs and butterfly-wings into their embroideries in India. The great hats flock; they shadow the pavement. And all the while *tran-tan-tan* above it dominates the band.

Little boys carrying sugar-canes eight feet long all hung with tiny flags add great colour to the scene. The canes are perforated with tiny holes, and in each hole is a sugar-plum mounted on a long match or wire, and each sugar plum has a tiny flag hanging from it. A dozen boys are carrying these resplendent poles; several others are carrying gourds perforated and adorned in the same way.

There are park seats all the way round, and there sit the more leisurely of the listeners and the tired, and watch the world go by. Old dames with trays of pineapple, and girls with baskets of pine kernels, go from seat to seat selling their wares.

The Zapotec women are straight as pine trees. They wear voluminous cotton skirts, but their feet are bare. Above the waist they do not mind how much of their bodies they expose; they wear commonly a slightly embroidered cotton vest cut as low as the rise of their bosoms and leaving their arms bare from just below the shoulders. They have broad open faces, carved mouths, lined brows, and an enormous flow of raven hair, which they allow to hang almost to their knees. They wear earrings of filigre gold, and beautiful gold chains round their bare necks. They may be on the point of beggary and yet wear these. The young ones are very beautiful, but quiet-eyed and never lascivious. They hold their heads so far back that if they wore hairpins and dropped one it would always fall clear of their bodies.

Outside the Palacio the sentries march to and fro with bayonets fixed and loaded rifles. The sergeant of the guard has golden bobbinettes hanging from six golden chevrons. At the changing of the guard bugles sound within the palace yard in a sort of counter blast to the triumphant choruses of brass coming from the branches of the palm trees and the electric lights of the bandstand. Oaxaca, birthplace of Diaz, birthplace of Juarez, is proud of itself and makes some show under the Mexican sky.

Round and round walks the crowd, and there mingle with the Indians American men and women, jaunty men dressed anyhow and women in low-cut evening gowns simpering to one another and to their male companions. Mexican belles also come out, with highly painted faces and dainty manicured hands. Girls in their teens join one another, and all holding arms walk in strings of sevens and eights. Youths of similar age walk in similar strings. Horsemen with tight trousers and silver spurs dismount and tie up their steeds and join the throng. The Governor himself, the legislature of the State, joins the parade. There is the highest and also the lowest. Bow, bow, bow, come the beggars. You give them centavos or you give them cakes. They wear old dusty sombreros of straw, and you put the cakes in the brim. You see beggars with dozens of cakes and *tortillas* and rolls in the brims of their straw sombreros. The blind beggars walk in tandems: blind mother led by seeing child, sister by sister, grandfather by grandson. There are two pseudo-beggars, too proud actually to beg, and they get more alms than all the rest. One is a magnificent fellow with a gigantic straw sombrero. He has lost both legs at the knee, but he must have been very handsome. He has large pads now like the wooden boots put on horses drawing the heavy roller over a lawn, and on these pads he walks like any other man, using hip muscles where we use the muscles of the knee. His yellow hat points backward from his head; he carries a boot-black's stool, and wherever he goes the crowd makes way for him—a king of the pavement and of all beggars and boot-blacks. The other pseudo-beggar is a boy with curved spine and twisted body. He walks on all-fours and has a basket of matches or sweets hung from his neck. All among the people he jumps like a frog—and whose heart can be so hard as to refuse him when he looks up with angel smile, so sweetly, so appealingly? You pretend to buy, he looks at what you give him, meditatively. He looks up at you, smiling, but perhaps a little troubled in expression.

" Adios? " he asks, as if it were a question.

" Adios," you reply.

The trouble clears from his face; he is perfectly happy.

" Adios, adios," he exclaims, and hops on like a frog amid the bare brown feet of the Indians and the polished boots of Mexicans and Americans.

Tran-tan-tan goes the band all the while, and the Zapotec bandmaster with narrowed waist and rigid little head and shoulders looks like Juarez himself. And the rattle of the gourds is like tambourines struck on the knees of dancing girls.   *Stephen Graham*

XLIV: HIGH-CHIN BOB

'Way high up in the Mokiones, among the mountain-
        tops,
A lion cleaned a yearlin's bones and licked his thank-
        ful chops;
When who upon the scene should ride, a-trippin'
        down the slope,
But High-Chin Bob of sinful pride and maverick-
        hungry rope.

"Oh, glory be to me!" says he, "an' Fame's unfadin'
        flowers,
I ride my good top-hoss to-day and I'm top hand of the
        Lazy-J,
So Kitty-cat, you're ours!"

The lion licked his paws so brown and dreamed soft
        dreams of veal,
As High-Chin's loop came circlin' down and roped
        him round his meal;

75

He yowled quick fury in the world and all the hills
    yelled back:
That top-hoss give a snort and whirled and Bob
    caught up his slack.

"Oh, glory be to me" says he, " we'll hit the glory trail,
No man has looped a lion's head and lived to drag the
    beggar dead,
Till I shall tell the tale."

'Way high up in the Mokiones that top-hoss done his
    best
'Mid whippin' brush and rattlin' stones from cañon-
    floor to crest;
Up and down and round and cross Bob pounded
    weak and wan,
But pride still glued him to his hoss and glory drove
    him on.

" Oh, glory be to me," says he, " this glory trail is rough,
I'll keep this dally round the horn until the toot of
    judgment morn,
Before I holler 'nough! "

Three suns had rode their circle home beyond the
    desert rim
And turned their star herds loose to roam the ranges
    high and dim,
And whenever Bob turned and hoped the limp
    remains to find,
A red-eyed lion, belly-roped, but healthy, loped
    behind!

" *Oh, glory be to me,*" says Bob, " *he kain't be drug to*
  death!
These heroes that I've read about were only fools that
  stuck it out
To the end of mortal breath! "

'Way high up in the Mokiones, if you ever come there
  at night,
You'll hear a ruckus amongst the stones that'll lift
  your hair with fright;
You'll see a cow-hoss thunder by and a lion trail
  along,
And the rider bold, with chin on high, sings forth his
  glory song:

" *Oh, glory be to me!* " says he, " *and to my mighty*
  noose!
Oh, pardner, tell my friends below I took a ragin' dream
  in tow,
And if I didn't lay him low—I never turned him loose! "
                                    Charles Badger Clark

XLV: THE RETIREMENT

Irregular stanzas, addressed to Mr. Izaak Walton

Farewell, thou busy world! and may
    We never meet again
Here I can eat, and sleep and pray,
And do more good in one short day,
Then he, who his whole age outwears
Upon the most conspicuous theatres,
Where nought but variety and vice do reign.

77

II

Good God! how sweet are all things here!
How beautiful the fields appear!
　　How cleanly do we feed and lie!
Lord! what good hours do we keep!
How quietly we sleep!
　　What peace! what unanimity
How innocent from the lewd fashion
Is all our business, all our recreation!

III

Oh, how happy here's our leisure!
Oh, how innocent our pleasure!
Oh, ye valleys! oh, ye mountains!
Oh, ye groves, and crystal fountains,
How I love at liberty,
By turns, to come and visit ye!

IV

Dear Solitude, the soul's best friend,
　　That man acquainted with himself dost make,
And all his Maker's wonders to extend,
With thee I here converse at will,
And would be glad to do so still,
For it is thou alone that keep'st the soul awake.

V

How calm and quiet a delight,
Is it, alone
To read and meditate and write,
　　By none offended and offending none!
To walk, ride, sit, or sleep at one's own ease,
And, pleasing a man's self, none other to displease.

78

VI

Oh, my beloved Nymph! fair Dove,
Princess of rivers! How I love
  Upon thy flowery banks to lie,
And view thy silver stream,
When gilded by a summer's beam!
  And in it, all thy wanton fry,
    Playing at liberty;
And, with my angle upon them,
  The all of treachery
  I ever learned industriously to try.

VII

Oh, my beloved rocks! that rise
To awe the earth and brave the skies:
From some aspiring mountains crown
  How dearly do I love,
Giddy with pleasure, to look down,
  And from the vale to view the noble heights
    above!

VIII

Oh my beloved caves! from Dog-star's heat,
And all anxieties my safe retreat;
What safety, privacy, what true delight,
  In th'artificial night,
Your gloomy entrails make,
Have I taken, do I take!
How oft when grief has made me fly
To hide me from society

Ev'n of my dearest friends, have I
  In your recesses' friendly shade
  All my sorrows open laid
And my most secret woes entrusted to your privacy.

IX

Lord! would men let me alone;
What an over-happy one
  Should I think myself to be,
Might I, in this denst place,
Which most men in discourse, disgrace,
  Live but undisturb'd and free!
Here, in this despised recess,
  Would I, maugre winter's cold,
And the summer's worst excess,
Try to live out to sixty full years old!
And, all the while,
  Without an envious eye,
On any thriving under Fortune's smile,
  Contented live, and then—contented die.

Charles Cotton

XLVI

These are the rules of the road:—
1. Keep away from the Cities.
2. Keep away from the railroads.
3. Have nothing to do with money and carry no baggage.
4. Ask for dinner about quarter after eleven.
5. Ask for supper, lodging and breakfast about quarter of five.
6. Travel alone.
7. Be neat, deliberate, chaste and civil.
8. Preach the Gospel of Beauty.

Vachel Lindsay

XLVII: THE GOSPEL OF BEAUTY

Being the new " creed of a beggar " by that vain and foolish mendicant Nicholas Vachel Lindsay, printed for his personal friends in his home village— Springfield, Illinois. It is his intention to carry this gospel across the country beginning June, 1912, returning in due time.

I come to you penniless and afoot, to bring a message. I am starting a new religious idea. The idea does not say "no" to any creed that you have heard. . . . After this, let the denomination to which you now belong be called in your heart " the church of beauty " or " the church of the open sky." . . .

The church of beauty has two sides: the love of beauty and the love of God.

The things most worth while are one's own hearth and neighbourhood. We should make our own home and neighbourhood the most democratic, the most beautiful and the holiest in the world. The children now growing up should become devout gardeners or architects or park architects or teachers of dancing in the Greek spirit or musicians or novelists or poets or story-writers or craftsmen or wood-carvers or dramatists or actors or singers. They should find their talent and nurse it industriously. They should believe in every possible application to art-theory of the thoughts of the Declaration of Independence and Lincoln's Gettysburg address. They should, if led by the spirit, wander over the whole nation in search of the secret of democratic beauty with their hearts at the same time filled to overflowing with the right-eousness of God. Then they should came back to their own hearth and neighbourhood and gather a little circle of their own sort of workers about them and strive to make the neighbourhood and home more beautiful and democratic and holy with their special art. . . . They should labour in their little circle expecting neither reward nor honours. . . . In their darkest hours they should be made strong by the vision of a completely beautiful neighbourhood and the passion for a completely democratic art. Their reason for living should be that joy in beauty which no wounds can take away, and that joy in the love of God which no crucifixion can end.

Vachel Lindsay

XLVIII: EMBLEMS OF TRAMPING

The fire is the altar of the open-air life. Its wandering smokes go upward like men's thoughts; its sparks are like human lives.

The coffee-pot is the emblem of conviviality.

The rough-hewn staff, the tramp's third leg, is the emblem of his will to jog on.

The knapsack, like Pilgrim's burden, is the confession of mortality, and of the load which every son of Adam carries on his shoulders.

Every door and gate which he sees means the *way out*, not the way in.

There are three emblems of life: the first is the open road, the second is the river, and the third is the wilderness. The road is the simplest of these emblems —with its milestones for years, its direction posts to show you the way, its inns for feasting, its churches for prayer, its cross-roads of destiny, its happy corners of love and meeting, its sad ones of bereavement and farewell; its backward vista of memory, its forward one of hope.

Life certainly is like a road, or a network of roads; like a highway for some, like a pleasant country road for others, like a crooked lane for some, like a path that bends back to its beginnings for most.

There is the narrow way of the Puritans, a passage between walls of righteousness; there is the broad way of the epicureans, so broad they mistake the breadth for the length and lose themselves on it. But, broad or narrow, the road seems inadequate as an emblem of the tramping life. There shall be roads in our life, but our life shall not be always in roads.

The road smacks rather of duty and purpose, of

utility, and of " getting there." Our penchant is to get off the road. I do not care to link tramping with utility. It may be good for the physical health, but that shall not be its object; it may be good for broadening the mind and deepening the sources of pleasure but these are not the goal. Tramping is a straying from the obvious. Even the crookedest road is sometimes too straight. You learn that it is artificial, that originally it was not made for mere tramping. Roads were made for armies and then for slaves and labourers, and for " transport." Few have been made for pleasure.

But was life merely meant for pleasure? Perhaps not. But it was meant for happiness or for the quest of happiness.

You are more likely to meet your enemies, if you have any, upon the road than off it. But then also you are more likely to meet friends there, too. You may seek your friends with success on the road. And if you wish counsel they are there to help you. " Life is like a road." says a Kirghiz proverb. " If you go astray it is not your enemies who will show you the way, but your friends."

Still, where the Kirghiz live, in Central Asia, there are few roads and you cannot go astray on them. The proverb must refer to mountain tracks. " Life is like a mountain track." Yes, that is better. Let the mountain track be our first emblem of life.

For the Sokols and the Scouts, the roads shall mean much more, because their lives are auxiliary to military efficiency. They learn to be ready to resist an enemy of their homeland. A good scout becomes a good volunteer soldier, a good route marcher. But scout and sokol are transitional. The scout movement is like a tug to take an ocean-going ship out of harbour.

There comes a point when the ship can make its own destiny under its own steam. The Scout and Guide movement helps boys and girls out of the rut of village life, starts them moving, and once set going, many of them keep moving all their lives, and never once stagnate. On the roads that lead out into the great world they march in their companies, with scoutmasters and commanders. Then the road is a glorious symbol of freedom and life.

The second emblem is the river, which, clear and innocent, finds the easiest and most charming way from birth to eternity. We were born on an invisible river which keeps gliding and singing and filling and flowing. We do not know where we go, but we know we are on the stream. We do not always perceive the movement, but we perceive that the landscape has changed.

So when we look on a river we are affected by its hidden relationship to our own life. The river interprets our mood. The road suggests God as a taskmaster who would have us work; the river suggests Him as a poet who would have us live in poetry. The Creator must be a poet—not a General or a Judge or a Master Builder; there is so much of pure poetry in His creation. The river, like a child's definition of a parable, is an earthly story with a heavenly meaning.

When we look on a river with a poet's eyes we see in it the reflection of an invisible river, the river of Time, the river of man's life, the river of Eternity. " Man may come and man may go, but I go on for ever."

There is a strange and wonderful vigilance about the river which rolls past us where we sleep in the grass, murmuring and calling the whole night long, something of the vigilance of the starry sky. You sleep, but an eternal sleepless sentry paces by all the while.

Then in the morning, when we bathe in the river, we are our own John the Baptists, out in the wilderness, baptising ourselves with water, and saying: " Repent, for the Kingdom of Heaven is at hand. Turn away from the road, for Heaven is near by." And we eat that wild honey of the wilderness, which the prophet ate when his baptising was done.

When we wash in the stream we are washing ourselves with life. When we swim in the stream, especially against the stream, we are joying the heart of an unseen Mother who takes pride in us all, knowing that, although we must at last flow out with the stream we can triumph over it for moments.

And, drinking from the stream, we partake of the water which flows from the mountain of God—Nature's communion cup.

The third emblem of life is the wilderness—that place to which wise men and poets and saints are driven in the last resort. " There is a pleasure in the pathless woods," wrote Byron. " There is society where none intrudes." The wilderness tells you more when you are attuned to it. That is seldom the experience of the tramp on his first long divagation from the beaten track. The wilderness tires him, the forests blind him, the mountains wear him down, the endless plain rises under him and smites his feet.

But there comes a point when there is a symmetry even in the wildest disarray of Nature, when man's symmetry of parks and garden cities and roads and rides is a poor joke, a strange aberration of the human mind.

The universe is a most complicated lock with innumerable wards and windings and combination numbers. If the starry sky at night is a lock—you would say there is no key in the world to fit it. No key in the world truly—but in the human heart somewhere there is a wonderful key. " Have I not in my bosom a key called ' Promise ' ? " said Pilgrim. When you find that key you can plunge it into the cunning aperture of Nature or Night. But you must know the combination numbers, and even then it will not turn if you do not first sing a verse of the Song of the Heart.

Quite a fairy tale—even so: Life is a fairy tale, one of a series, like the *Arabian Nights*. And if it is a fairy tale rather than what Darwin and Herbert Spencer and Einstein have averred, how much more important to us all the fairy tale becomes.

Fairy tales are begun in the midst of woods, in strange forgotten glades, and at moments between dawn and the morning, and sunset and night.

" Fairy tales," wrote Novalis, " are dreams of our homeland—which is everywhere and nowhere." And to be everywhere and nowhere at the same time means to be in the wilds, and preferably quite lost. The absolute tramp, whom, I may say, I have never met, is a man with no address, no card, no reliable passport no recognisable finger-prints. But of course he is no ape-man, no Tarzan, or son of Tarzan. Choice, not accident, leads him to the wilds.

The starry sky is the emblem of home, the highest roof in the universe. The sun is the mind, by whose light man seeks his way; the moon is the reflection of the mind on the heart, and is the emblem of melancholy and poetry.

88

However, of all these emblems, the coffee-pot is apt to be the most real and vital. You will be on your knees morning and evening before your altar fire abasing your brow and blowing the flames which are beneath it. Sun, moon, forest, river, road—these pass, but the coffee-pot remains. It is so in life generally, and the tramp, however much a poet he may be, is a mortal like the rest of us. The moon may be hidden by a cloud, but that is not nearly so calamitous as having left the coffee-pot at the last resting-place. *Stephen Graham*

XLIX: CREED OF THE CAMP FIRE GIRLS

THE WOOD-GATHERER'S DESIRE

As faggots are brought from the forest,
Firmly held by the sinews that bind them,
I will cleave to my Camp Fire Sisters,
Wherever, whenever, I find them,
I will strive to grow strong like the pine tree,
To be pure in my deepest desire,
To be true to the truth that is in me,
And follow the law of the fire.

THE FIRE-MAKER'S DESIRE

As fuel is brought to the fire,
So I purpose to bring my strength,
My ambition,
My heart's desire,
My joy,
And my sorrows
To the fire of humankind.
For I will tend

As my fathers have tended,
And my father's fathers
Since time began,
The fire that is called
The love of man for man,
The love of man for God.

THE TORCH-BEARER'S DESIRE

That light which has been given to me
I desire to pass undimmed to others.

RE-DEDICATION

I believe in the future,
I believe, therefore, in to-day,
And I try to make my life
A joy to myself and
A pleasure to those about me.
I realise the destiny within me;
I try to find the beautiful in life,
And where it is not, I create beauty.
I feel my responsibility as a citizen of a great nation;
I feel my glory as one of the mothers of the new
        generation,
Which with new eyes and steadier steps
Will reach the high places that now
Are but a purple haze on the horizon.
I believe in the new womanhood
Which combines the beauty of the old womanhood
With citizenship and social consciousness.
I know I am, and hold within me the promise of the
        future.
I realise my responsibility,
I do not flinch nor falter;
I am a Camp Fire Girl.

L: ON GOING A JOURNEY

One of the pleasantest things in the world is going a journey; but I like to go by myself. I can enjoy society in a room; but out of doors, nature is company enough for me. I am then never less alone than when alone.

> " The fields his study, nature was his book."

I cannot see the wit of walking and talking at the same time. When I am in the country, I wish to vegetate like the country. I am not for criticising hedge-rows and black cattle. I go out of town in order to forget the town and all that is in it. There are those who for this purpose go to watering-places, and carry the metropolis with them. I like more elbow-room, and fewer incumbrances. I like solitude, when I give myself up to it, for the sake of solitude; nor do I ask for—

> " a friend in my retreat,
> Whom I may whisper solitude is sweet."

The soul of a journey is liberty, perfect liberty, to think, feel, do just as one pleases. We go a journey chiefly to be free of all impediments and of all in-conveniences; to leave ourselves behind, much more to get rid of others. It is because I want a little breathing-space to muse on indifferent matters, where Contemplation

> " May plume her feathers and let grow her wings,
> That in the various bustle of resort
> Were all too ruffled, and sometimes impair'd,"

that I absent myself from the town for awhile, with-out feeling at a loss the moment I am left by myself. Instead of a friend in a post-chaise or in a Tilbury, to exchange good things with, and vary the same stale topics over again, for once let me have a truce with impertinence. Give me the clear blue sky over my head, and the green turf beneath my feet, a winding road before me, and a three hours march to dinner— and then to thinking! It is hard if I cannot start some game on these lone heaths. I laugh, I run, I leap, I sing for joy. From the point of yonder rolling cloud, I plunge into my past being and revel there, as the sun-burnt Indian plunges headlong into the wave that wafts him to his native shore. Then long-forgotten things, like " sunken wrack and sumless treasuries " burst upon my eager sight, and I begin to feel, think, and be myself again. Instead of an awkward silence, broken by attempts at wit or dull commonplaces, mine is that undisturbed silence of the heart which alone is perfect eloquence. No one likes puns, alliterations, antithesis, argument, and analysis better than I do; but I sometimes had rather be without them. "Leave, oh, leave me to my repose!" I have just now other business in hand, which would seem idle to you, but is with me " very stuff of the conscience." Is not this wild rose sweet without a comment? Does not this daisy leap to my heart set in its coat of emerald? Yet if I were to explain to you the circumstance that has so endeared it to me, you would only smile. Had I not better then keep it to myself, and let it serve me to brood over, from here to yonder craggy point, and from thence onward to the far-distant horizon? I should be but bad company all that way, and therefore prefer being alone. I have heard it said that you may, when the moody fit comes on, walk or ride by yourself, and indulge your reveries. But this looks like a breach of manners, a neglect of others, and you are thinking all the time that you ought to rejoin your party. " Out upon such half-faced fellowship," say I. I like to be either entirely to myself, or entirely at the disposal of others; to talk or be silent, to walk or sit still, to be sociable or solitary. I was pleased with an observation of Mr. Cobbett's, that " he thought it a bad French custom to drink our wine with our meals, and that an Englishman ought only to do one thing at a time." So I cannot talk and think, or indulge in melancholy musing and lively conversation by fits and starts. " Let me have a companion of my way," says Sterne, " were it but to remark how the shadows lengthen as the sun declines." It is beautifully said; but in my opinion this continual comparing of notes interferes with the involuntary impression of the things upon the mind, and hurts the sentiment. If you only hint what you feel in a kind of dumb show, it is insipid; if you have to explain it, it is making a toil of a pleasure. You cannot read the book of nature without being put perpetually to the trouble of translating it for the benefit of others. I am for the synthetical method on a journey, in preference to the analytical. I am content to lay in a stock of ideas then, and to examine and anatomise them afterwards. I want to see my vague notions float like the down of the thistle before the breeze, and not to have them entangled in the briars and thorns of controversy. For once I like to have it all my own way; and this is impossible unless you are alone, or in such company as I do not covet. I have no objection to argue a point with anyone for twenty miles of measured road, but not for pleasure. If you remark the scent of a beanfield crossing the road, perhaps your fellow-traveller has no smell. If you point to a distant object, perhaps he is short-sighted, and has to take out his glass to look at it. There is a feeling in the air, a tone in the colour of a cloud which hits your fancy, but the effect of which you are unable to account for. There is then no sympathy, but an uneasy craving after it, and a dissatisfaction which pursues you on the way, and in the end probably produces ill-humour. Now I never quarrel with myself, and take all my own conclusions for granted till I find it necessary to defend them against objections.

．　．　．　．　．

There is hardly anything that shows the short-sightedness or capriciousness of the imagination more than travelling does. With change of place we change our ideas; nay, our opinions and feelings. We can by an effort indeed transport ourselves to old and long-forgotten scenes, and then the picture of the mind revives again; but we forget those that we have just left. It seems that we can think but of one place at a time. The canvas of the fancy is but of a certain extent, and if we paint one set of objects upon it, they immediately efface every other. We cannot enlarge our conceptions, we only shift our point of view. The landscape bares its bosom to the enraptured eye, we take our fill of it, and seem as if we could form no other image of beauty or grandeur. We pass on, and think no more of it: the horizon that shuts it from our sight also blots it from our memory like a dream. In travelling through a wild barren country, I can form no idea of a woody and cultivated one. It appears to me that all the world must be barren, like what I see of it. In the country we forget the town, and in town we despise the country. " Beyond Hyde

94

Park," says Sir Fopling Flutter, " all is a desert." All that part of the map that we do not see before us is a blank. The world in our conceit of it is not much bigger than a nutshell. It is not one prospect expanded into another, county joined to county, kingdom to kingdom, lands to seas, making an image voluminous and vast; the mind can form no larger idea of space than the eye can take in at a single glance. The rest is a name written in a map, a calculation of arithmetic. For instance, what is the true signification of that immense mass of territory and population, known by the name of China to us? An inch of pasteboard on a wooden globe, of no more account than a China orange! Things near us are seen of the size of life: things at a distance are diminished to the size of the understanding. We measure the universe by ourselves, and even comprehend the texture of our own being only piecemeal. In this way, however, we remember an infinity of things and places. The mind is like a mechanical instrument that plays a great variety of tunes, but it must play them in succession. One idea recalls another, but it at the same time excludes all others. In trying to renew old recollections, we cannot as it were unfold the web of our existence; we must pick out the single threads. So in coming to a place where we have formerly lived and with which we have intimate associations, every one must have found that the feeling grows more vivid the nearer we approach the spot, from the mere anticipation of the actual impression: we remember circumstances, feelings, persons, places, names, that we had not thought of for years; but for the time all the rest of the world is forgotten!

To return to the question I have quitted above.

I have no objection to see ruins, aqueducts, pictures, in company with a friend or a party, but rather the contrary, for the former reason reversed. They are intelligible matters, and will bear talking about. The sentiment here is not tacit, but communicable and overt. Salisbury Plain is barren of criticism, but Stonehenge will bear a discussion antiquarian, picturesque, and philosophical. In setting out on a party of pleasure, the first consideration always is where we shall go to; in taking a solitary ramble, the question is what we shall meet with by the way. " The mind is its own place "; nor are we anxious to arrive at the end of our journey. I can myself do the honours indifferently well to works of art and curiosity. I once took a party to Oxford with no mean *éclat*—shewed them that seat of the Muses at a distance,

" With glistering spires and pinnacles adorned"—descanted on the learned air that breathes from the grassy quadrangles and stone walls of halls and colleges—was at home in the Bodleian; and at Blenheim quite superseded the powdered Ciceroni that attended us, and that pointed in vain with his wand to commonplace beauties in matchless pictures. As another exception to the above reasoning, I should not feel confident in venturing on a journey in a foreign country without a companion. I should want at intervals to hear the sound of my own language. There is an involuntary antipathy in the mind of an Englishman to foreign manners and notions that requires the assistance of social sympathy to carry it off. As the distance from home increases, this relief, which was at first a luxury, becomes a passion and an appetite. A person would almost feel stifled to find himself in the deserts of Arabia without friends and countrymen: there must be allowed to be something in the view of Athens or old Rome that claims the utterance of speech; and I own that the Pyramids are too mighty for any single contemplation. In such situations, so opposite to all one's ordinary train of ideas, one seems a species by one's self, a limb torn off from society, unless one can meet with instant fellowship and support. Yet I did not feel this want or craving very . pressing once, when I first set my foot on the laughing shores of France. Calais was peopled with novelty and delight. The confused, busy murmur of the place was like oil and wine poured into my ears; nor did the mariners' hymn, which was sung from the top of an old crazy vessel in the harbour, as the sun went down, send an alien sound into my soul. I only breathed the air of general humanity. I walked over " the vine-covered hills and gay regions of France," erect and satisfied; for the image of man was not cast down and chained to the foot of arbitrary thrones: I was at no loss for language, for that of all the great schools of painting was open to me. The whole is vanished like a shade. Pictures, heroes, glory, freedom, all are fled: nothing remains but the Bourbons and the French people! There is undoubtedly a sensation in travelling into foreign parts that is to be had nowhere else; but it is more pleasing at the time than lasting. It is too remote from our habitual associations to be a common topic of discourse or reference, and, like a dream or another state of existence, does not piece into our daily modes of life. It is an animated but a momentary hallucination. It demands an effort to exchange our actual for our ideal identity; and to feel the pulse of our old transports revive very keenly, we must " jump " all our present comforts and con-

H

nexions. Our romantic and itinerant character is not to be domesticated. Dr. Johnson remarked how little foreign travel added to the facilities of conversation in those who had been abroad. In fact, the time we have spent there is both delightful and in one sense instructive; but it appears to be cut out of our substantial, downright existence, and never to join kindly on to it. We are not the same, but another, and perhaps more enviable individual, all the time we are out of our own country. We are lost to ourselves, as well as our friends. So the poet somewhat quaintly sings,

" Out of my country and myself I go."

Those who wish to forget painful thoughts, do well to absent themselves for awhile from the ties and objects that recall them; but we can be said only to fulfil our destiny in the place that gave us birth. I should on this account like well enough to spend the whole of my life in travelling abroad, if I could anywhere borrow another life to spend afterwards at home!

William Hazlitt

LI: A HOLIDAY ON TRAMP

For most holidays many preparations are necessary, for a walking one these are reduced to a minimum. For one thing the time of year makes little difference, and the weather does not make much, for the open air to my mind is always enjoyable. To this I attribute in part the cheerfulness of my disposition. I was once rallied by a friend on being a non-smoker, and was told that I should find a cigar a great cure for worry. But I never worry. A writer on Australia has said that the cheerful faces of the people there are due to their never having to worry about what sort of a day it is going to be. An Englishman has no sooner planned a day's excursion, or an afternoon's picnic, or a fortnight at the seaside, than he is tormented with anxiety lest it should rain. I have no such fears. It is true that fine mornings may become overclouded, but then on the wettest days the sun may break through, and, as Charles the Second said, there are but few days when an Englishman cannot enjoy himself out of doors.

The best preparation for a walking holiday lies not in fine weather so much as in hard feet, and to get the feet hard there is but one way, and that is by walking. I have never found any other method effectual. I have been recommended to soap my stockings, to use Fuller's earth, and so on, but the best method, to my mind, is to walk the feet hard and then leave them to take care of themselves. If the day be wet, or the ground soft, then two pennyworth of whisky poured into the shoes will afford the greatest relief against the discomforts of wet feet.

What is it necessary to take? Remember that every ounce tells, and if your burden is too heavy the enjoyment of the walk will be diminished. Very few people in these days can understand Bunyan's allusion to Christian and his burden, and the relief it was to get rid of it. But I have known what it was to toil up Snowdon with too much luggage on my back, which effectually spoilt even such a walk as that. So I advise as little as possible, a single change of shirt and stockings, brushes, comb, razor, and other necessary impedimenta, with the single luxury of a pair of slippers will suffice. The perspiration and the dust will no doubt make you sigh for clean things, and these can easily be obtained by washing your garments in the hand basin of the inn and hanging them out of the window to dry.

I advise that you go without an overcoat, for your difficulty will never be how to get warm, but how to keep cool. An umbrella is as easily carried as a stick, and is more useful. Dismiss from your mind any fancies that a thick stick would come in useful in case you meet a robber. Such people lie in wait at street corners for tipsy men or unprotected women, and do not waste their time on country roads, where few but penniless tramps are to be met. Indeed, you must not be surprised or offended if you find yourself taken for a poor fellow who walks because he cannot afford to ride. I once was accosted on the road by a poor man who sought to excite my sympathy by saying he did not know where he was going to sleep that night. I truthfully replied that I was in similar case, whereupon he said if I was down on my luck he would share his bit of 'bacca with me. I took it, and have tied a piece of ribbon round it as a memento of the nearest approach to the widow's mite I ever knew.

You will do well to have a goal to walk to, otherwise your walking is apt to be on the same lines as that of Mark Twain, who, as he always found a train just starting for the place he was going to, took the easier way of getting there. You will always find an excuse ready to hand for not walking, if you want one. You will do well, therefore, to do as I do, and register a vow not to get into a railway train.

If it is the first time you have undertaken a long walk, I would suggest one to London for a start. For one thing the road is sure to be easy to find, and I have noticed that there are relics enough of the old coaching days in the shape of good inns at easy distances to ensure good, light refreshments on the way and a good bed for the night.

No matter where you start from, make out your road, perhaps to Land's End or John o' Groats, through the cathedral cities of England, or to Ben Nevis, no matter where, but reckon you will do 150 miles a week. For the first day's walk look out a place 25 miles distant, and depend upon it the distance will be farther than you think.

My experience tells me that the reason why so many pedestrians give up is because they do too much at first. I know that you cannot always limit yourself, as stopping places won't locate themselves just where you want them. Once I had to walk 42 miles before I reached a bed, and once (in Ireland) I walked 40 miles and did not reach a bed then, but had to lie on the chairs of a railway waiting-room. In England, however, you can generally depend on a bed within a mile or two. I always try and choose an inn where I see signs of company. It is a rough-and-ready proof that a place is good if it is patronised, and after walking all day by yourself you will want some cheerful companions.

Nobody can appreciate the delights of walking save those who experience them. What with hours in the open air, the body always in motion, the muscles taking exercise, and then the rests and the meals which you feel you have earned, all combine to make a satisfied mind. No cold nor chill, nor ache nor pain, can survive a few hours' walking, and all one's cares and worries go the same way. But especially do I commend the freedom of the road to those who, like myself, are condemned to wear black cloth, white collars and cuffs, to sit down to dinner with serviettes and finger glasses, and generally to be *en grand tenue*. We know it is an artificial life, and consequently it is all the more enjoyable to return to Nature and her ways. Nothing comes amiss to a man on a walking tour. Those who at home cannot eat veal or new bread, or drink beer, find that their digestion can master anything. People who do much brain work are often cursed with sleeplessness, but if any sufferer fails to be cured by a walking tour I shall be astonished. Pale people, when they look in the glass, will be astonished to find what a colour they have, and indeed all the world seems to smile when a man is in health and condition.

A most important matter with nine people out of ten, when going for a holiday, is the question of expense. I always think when I am tramping through unfrequented roads that I come nearer to the solution of how to live on sixpence a day than at any other time. Dwellers in towns, and those who pursue the beaten track, such as a visit to the seaside, to the lakes, to Chatsworth, and the like, find it hard to believe that there are any people in the world so unsophisticated as not to have learnt how to charge. I know, also, that I put a strain on the credulity of my readers when I mention the amount of some of my bills. The total charge does not seem sufficient to cover the prime cost of the victuals consumed, let alone house room and kitchen fire. Thus, perched on the top of the high ground between Whitby and Saltburn is an inn where I stopped one day for dinner. I was invited to help myself to a sirloin of beef, and had vegetables, apple-tart and cream, and cheese. I was charged one shilling. When I went over the Buttertubs Pass, between Swaledale and Wensleydale, I stopped overnight at Muker, which meant supper and breakfast, as well as a bed, and when I asked for my bill next morning the honest woman said she could not write, and her little girl (who was a scholar) had gone to school, besides she had no paper, but if I would give her a couple of shillings she would be thankful. Once when walking to St. David's I had tea at an inn about six miles from Haverfordwest, and was charged fourpence halfpenny for a meal which included a jug of cream, a cake, and two pots of jam, beside the staple articles of a tea-table.

Lest it should be thought that what I took " for the good of the house " made amends, and that what they did not get in meal they got in malt, I may mention that I am a total abstainer.

I should like to emphasise the fact that all my walks have been done for the love of the thing. I have never had a bet or a wager on the subject, and I was never under any obligation to walk a step farther than I chose. Yet, for the mere delight of the thing, I have performed long continental walks to Rome, Venice, Monte Carlo, and even to Buda-Pesth, and have walked across Ireland, and from Yorkshire to Ben Nevis, and through Wales, besides exploring every county in England. I have been nearly lost amid the snows of Norway, and melted under the sun of Italy, and starved in the wilds of Ireland, and yet I never return from a tramp without a longing to be off again, and I never am free from " the tickles in my feet," as a navvy describes the promptings to change his job.

It is very hard to recommend a walking tour to any particular place, as people are governed by the length of time at their disposal, and their place of abode, as well as by their powers of endurance. But I have no hesitation in saying, Let the tramp be over moorland or high ground, and on unfrequented roads if economy is necessary. Among things not generally known is that our present King was taken by his tutor, Mr. Tarver, for a walking tour, and His Majesty has been heard to declare that he learnt more from it than from his lesson books. It is an education, and fixes on the mind the course of rivers, the position of towns, and the relative heights of mountains, in a way that no book can do. It is an infallible cure for low spirits and the " blues," and teaches one what a deal of kindliness and good humour there is in the world, only waiting for us to enjoy it.

A. N. Cooper
(The Walking Parson)

LII: BARE FEET

The children too, especially the girls, some almost as tall as their large mothers, though still in short frocks, were very fine. The one pastime of these was paddling, and it was a delight to see their bare feet and legs. The legs of those who had been longest on the spot—probably several weeks in some instances— were of a deep nutty-brown hue suffused with pink;

after these a gradation of colour, light brown tinged with buff, pinkish buff and cream, like the Gloire de Dijon rose: and so on to the delicate tender pink of the clover blossom; and finally the purest ivory white of the latest arrivals whose skins had not yet been caressed and coloured by sun and wind.

How beautiful are the feet of these girls by the sea who bring us glad tidings of a better time to come and the day of a nobler courage, a freer, larger life when garments which have long oppressed and hindered shall have been cast away!

W. H. Hudson

LIII: SORE FEET

Thirty miles a day! It may have been noticed that among the contents of my satchel no mention was made of any remedy for sore feet, such as vaseline, Fuller's earth, etc. Like Hamlet, I " throw physic to the dogs," and let my feet take care of themselves. In my early walking-days I was often tempted to dip them in brooks and streams, forgetful how water makes them tender, and my first work at the end of the day's walk was to plunge them into a foot-bath just when they were most tender. But now I have a remedy which I borrowed of a Scotch professor. He taught me to pour whisky into my socks instead of down my throat, making the foot, shoe, and sock yielding and pliable. I give this as a sovereign preventive of sore feet.

A. N. Cooper
(The Walking Parson)

LIV: ADVICE TO MOUNTAINEERS

Don't climb slopes on the toes: place the boot flat and firmly, never lift higher than necessary. Take short steps. On steep slopes zigzagging is often of great help. For level going develop a good long, easy, swinging stride with knees slightly bent.

On a long " slog " a rough stick cut by the wayside, which can be discarded when rocks are reached, is both a help and a companion. An idea has arisen in this country that it is incorrect mountaineering to carry a stick. This is quite a mistake, as can be shown by the practice in other countries.

The secret of rapid and comfortable progress down steep slopes is to keep the knees well bent and to cultivate an easy swing of the body from the waist. It is often necessary to descend very steep and rough ground at full speed. Practise until you can do it with confidence at a fast run. A short stick trailed behind is found by some to be a great help in descending steep slopes.

Do not be disheartened if you are " nervy " or giddy near a drop; this will disappear if rocks are taken by gradually increasing difficulty and under proper leadership. On the rocks the rule is " slow and sure." The movements resemble those of a chameleon; feet are for climbing, hands for steadying and retaining the balance. Face the rock; do not release a hold until certain that the next permits retention of balance; retain three holds at a time as far as possible, and distribute the weight over the holds; never jerk or jump. Look out for unsound rock; test chock stones in a gully and a chimney. Avoid difficult climbs in rain, and beware always of wet rock; use rubber shoes on difficult rock when dry. Learn to belay the rope; belay on traverses and take short steps, don't cross the feet. One member of a party only is roped at a time; learn the correct knots before you start. If you are holding the rope " feel " your man the whole time. Be prepared for a slip; never release vigilance or care on the easiest climb. Never climb wearing a rucksac on difficult rocks; keep clear of rucksacs when being hauled up; *never climb alone*.

When you are soaked to the skin in cold, wet weather and a change or continued exercise is impossible, e.g. in a railway carriage, the circulation and warmth may be retained by friction. Rub the clothing and limbs and both will remain warm and the former will dry quickly.

Sitting on damp ground or cold rocks is inadvisable. Use sweater, rucksac or newspaper.

When walking in rain, keep the brim of felt hat turned up at the back and down at the front. This will divert much water from trickling down the spine.

If hopelessly lost in a mist or rain, avoid climbing up or down all rocks, even the most innocent looking. Keep your head; if darkness is approaching seek shelter of bush or rock. Keep your party together; collect firewood; resign yourselves quickly and quietly to a night out; keep cheerful.

D. Gordon Mills

Some years ago, while still an undergraduate, I chanced to be present at an informal gathering in which the conversation turned to confessions of respective aspirants.

" If only I had a few thousands," sighed a senior, " I'd make a trip around the world."

" Modest ambition! " retorted a junior. " But you'd better file it away for future reference, till you have made the money."

" With all due respect to bank accounts," I observed, " I believe a man with a bit of energy and good health could start *without* money and make a journey around the globe."

Laughter assailed the suggestion; yet as time rolled on I found myself often musing over that hastily conceived notion. Travel for pleasure has ever been considered a special privilege of the wealthy. That a man without ample funds should turn tourist seems to his fellow-beings an action little less reprehensible than an attempt to finance a corporation on worthless paper. He who would see the world, and has not been provided the means thereto by a considerate ancestor, should sit close at home until his life-work is done, his fortune made. Then let him travel; when his eyes have grown too dim to catch the beauty of a distant landscape, when struggle and experience have rendered him blasé and unimpressionable.

A spirit of rebellion against this traditional notion suggested a problem worthy of investigation. What would befall the man who set out to girdle the globe as the farmer's boy sets out to seek his fortune in the neighbouring city; on the alert for every opportunity, yet scornful of the fact that every foot of the way has not been paved before him? , ...

It was not until a year after my graduation that opportunity and my plans were ripe. I resolved to take a " year off," to wander through as much of the world as possible, and to return to my desk in the autumn, fifteen months later. As to my equipment for such a venture: I spoke French and German readily, Spanish and Italian with some fluency; I had " worked my way " on shorter journeys, had earned wages at a dozen varieties of manual labour in my own country, and had crossed the Atlantic once as a cattle man and once before the mast. It was my original intention to attempt the journey without money, without weapons, and without carrying baggage or supplies; to depend both for protection and the necessities of life on personal endeavour and the native resources of each locality. That plan I altered in one particular. I decided to carry a Kodak; and to obviate the necessity of earning *en route* what I might choose to squander in photography, I set out with a sum that seemed sufficient to cover that extraneous expense; to be exact: with one hundred and four dollars. As was to be expected, I spent this reserve fund early, in those countries of Northern Europe in which I had not planned an extensive stay. But the conditions of the self-imposed test were not thereby materially altered; for before the journey ended I had spent in photography, from my earnings, more than the original amount—to be exact again: one hundred and thirteen dollars.

The chief object of investigation being the masses, I made no attempt during the journey to rise above the estate of the common labourer. My plan included no fixed itinerary. The details of route I left to chance and the exigencies of circumstances. Yet this random wandering brought me to as many famous spots as any victim of a " personally conducted tour " could demand; and in addition, to many corners unknown to the regular tourist.

The question that aroused my curiosity has been answered: A man *can* girdle the globe without money, weapons, or baggage.

Harry A. Franck

LVI

Ho, every one that thirsteth, come ye to the waters, and he that hath no money; come ye, buy, and eat; yea, come, buy wine and milk without money and without price.

Wherefore do ye spend money for that which is not bread? and your labour for that which satisfieth not? hearken diligently unto me, and eat ye that which is good, and let your soul delight itself in fatness.

Incline your ear, and come unto me: hear, and your soul shall live; and I will make an everlasting covenant with you, even the sure mercies of David.

.   .   .   .   .

Seek ye the Lord while he may be found, call ye upon him while he is near:

Let the wicked forsake his way, and the unrighteous man his thoughts: and let him return unto the Lord, and he will have mercy upon him; and to our God, for he will abundantly pardon.

For my thoughts are not your thoughts, neither are your ways my ways, saith the Lord.

For as the heavens are higher than the earth, so are my ways higher than your ways, and my thoughts than your thoughts.

For as the rain cometh down, and the snow from heaven, and returneth not thither, but watereth the earth, and maketh it bring forth and bud, that it may give seed to the sower, and bread to the eater:

So shall my word be that goeth forth out of my mouth: it shall not return unto me void, but it shall accomplish that which I please, and it shall prosper in the thing whereto I sent it.

For ye shall go out with joy, and be led forth with peace: the mountains and the hills shall break forth before you into singing, and all the trees of the field shall clap their hands.

Instead of the thorn shall come up the fir tree, and instead of the brier shall come up the myrtle tree: and it shall be to the Lord for a name, for an everlasting sign that shall not be cut off.

Isaiah lv.

LVII

This book, it chalketh out before thine eyes
The man that seeks the everlasting prize:
It shows you whence he comes, whither he goes;
What he leaves undone; also what he does;
It also shows you how he runs and runs,
Till he unto the Gate of Glory comes.

It shows, too, who set out for life amain,
As if the lasting crown they would obtain.
Here also you may see the reason why
They lose their labour, and like fools do die.

This book will make a traveller of thee,
If by its counsel thou wilt ruled be.

John Bunyan

LVIII

Othello speaks:
Ancient, conduct them: you best know the place.
And, till she come, as truly as to heaven
I do confess the vices of my blood,
So justly to your grave ears I'll present
How I did thrive in this fair lady's love,
And she in mine.

   Her father loved me; oft invited me;
Still question'd me the story of my life,
From year to year, the battles, sieges, fortunes,
That I have pass'd.
I ran it through, even from my boyish days,
To the very moment that he bad me tell it:
Wherein I spake of most disastrous chances,
Of moving accidents by flood and field,
Of hair-breadth scapes i' the imminent deadly breach,
Of being taken by the insolent foe
And sold to slavery, of my redemption thence
And portance in my travels' history:
Wherein of antres vast and deserts idle,
Rough quarries, rocks and hills whose heads touch
    heaven,
It was my hint to speak—such was the process:
And of the Cannibals that each other eat,
The Anthropophagi and men whose heads
Do grow beneath their shoulders. This to hear
Would Desdemona seriously incline:
But still the house-affairs would draw her thence:
Which ever as she could with haste dispatch,
She'ld come again, and with a greedy ear
Devour up my discourse: which I observing,
Took once a pliant hour, and found good means

To draw from her a prayer of earnest heart
That I would all my pilgrimage dilate,
Whereof by parcels she had something heard,
But not intentively: I did consent,
And often did beguile her of her tears,
When I did speak of some distressful stroke
That my youth suffered. My story being done,
She gave me for my pains a world of sighs:
She swore, in faith, 'twas strange, 'twas passing
    strange,
'Twas pitiful, 'twas wondrous pitiful:
She wish'd she had not heard it, yet she wish'd
That heaven had made her such a man: she thank'd
    me,
And bade me, if I had a friend that loved her,
I should but teach him how to tell my story,
And that would woo her. Upon this hint I spake:
She loved me for the dangers I had pass'd,
And I loved her that she did pity them.
This only is the witchcraft I have used.

William Shakespeare

LIX: IN HONDURAS

One of the chief difficulties of the road in Honduras
is the impossibility of arousing the lazy inhabitants in
time to prepare some suggestion of breakfast at a
reasonably early hour. For to set off without eating
may be to fast all the hot and laborious day. The sun
was already warm when I took up the task of picking
my way from among the many narrow, red, labyrin-
thian paths that scattered over the hill on which San
Augustin reposes and radiated into the rocky, pine-

forested, tumbled mountain world surrounding it. Someone had said the trail to Santa Rosa was easy and comparatively level. But such words have strange meanings in Honduras. Not once during the day did there appear a level space ten yards in length. Hour after hour a narrow path, one of a score in which to go astray, worn in the whitish rock of a tumbled and irregular series of soft sandstone ridges with thin forests of pine or fir, clambered and sweated up and down incessantly by slopes steeper than any stairway, until I felt like the overworked chambermaid of a tall but elevatorless hotel. My foot was much swollen, and to make things worse the region was arid and waterless. Once I came upon a straggling mud village, but though it was half hidden by banana and orange groves not even fruit could be bought. Yet a day or two before some scoundrel had passed this way eating oranges constantly and strewing the trail with the tantalising peelings; a methodical, selfish, bourgeois fellow, who had not had the humane carelessness to drop a single fruit on all his gluttonous journey.

When I came at last, at the bottom of a thigh-straining descent, upon the first stream of the day, it made up for the aridity behind, for the path had eluded me and left me to tear through the jungle and wade a quarter-mile before I picked up the trail again. Refreshed, I began a task before which I might have turned back had I seen it all at once. Four mortal waterless hours I toiled steeply upward, more than twenty times sure I had reached the summit, only to see the trail, like some will-o'-the-wisp, draw on ahead unattainably in a new direction. I had certainly ascended four thousand feet when I threw myself down at last among the pines of the wind-swept summit. A draught from the gourd of a passing peon gave me new life for the corresponding descent. Several of these fellow-roasters now appeared, courteous fellows, often with black mustaches and imperial à la Napoleon III, who raised their hats and greeted me with a sing-song " Que se vaya bien," yet seemed remarkably stupid and perhaps a trifle treacherous. At length, well on in the afternoon, the road broke through a cutting and disclosed the welcome sight of the town of Santa Rosa, its white church bulking above all else built by man; the first suggestion of civilisation I had seen in Honduras.

Harry A. Franck

LX: DAWN IN THE CAUCASUS

I found a bush, and just after sunset, when the gnats sang in their mournful chorus, I made my bed. I was soon deep snuggled in my waterproof sleeping-sack—my dear old friend—night sharer of so many vicissitudes and slumbers. A wisp of *crêpe de Chine* about my head, I feared not the meanest of all foes, the mosquitoes that range two to each hair on the head. I know what happened as the darkness deepened: the birds slunk to sleep in the bushes, all save the night-jars and the owls that gurgled and hooted among the pines and maples. The dark moths flitted to and fro in the first breathless darkness of the summer night, the large red ants carried off on their backs the dead gnats that had perished at my hands at supper-time. Then the pale full moon arose out of a depth of soft white cloud—passionless, perfect. Still the owls hooted as I fell asleep. The night passed. Morning came and I arose gaily. Naught of what the hillman suggested had come to pass; only once had I started, and that at the touch of the wet snout of an inquisitive hedgehog. I remember now how piggy scuttled off. But two minutes after that I was sleeping again. There had been one other event of the night. About two hours before dawn the rain came softly down. A broad cloud had gently breasted this little mountain upon which I was encamped. It rained steadily and much. I curled myself more completely within my sack and let it rain. In the little moments when I did not sleep I heard the drops falling on the cover above me. Had any wild robber come upon this strange bundle under the bush his woodlore must have told him it was no beast or bird ever seen upon the hills or under the sky. I think he would have crossed himself and passed by.

So passed the first night of my tramp in the mountains, quite a unique night, soft, strange, wonderful. I felt I had begun a new life. I had entered into a new world and come into communion with Nature in a way as yet unknown.

The rain had stopped as the first light came up into the sky. I arose gaily, pleasantly cool and fit after the sleep and the rain. By the faint light I saw the valley below me, and the grand grey rocks on the other side. I looked up to the summit of my own mountain, and as I munched a remainder of dry bread felt all the unspeakable delight of an awakening with the birds after having spent the night with the mountains. But, indeed, I had awakened before the birds, and as yet the mountains slept, the long grey line of bearded warriors, calm, majestic, unmoved, invincible. Nature in reverence lay hushed beneath them, waiting for a signal. I passed carefully over the wet grasses—softly, secretly, as if everywhere children slept.

Clamber, clamber, clamber, up then to the highest point. At last I stood there with the dew on my heels. All the east lay before me, and such a horizon as one can only see when looking from the northern spurs of the Caucasus. The sun had not risen, and from north to south lay an illimitable length of deep blood-red, blood without life, red without light—dead, fearful, unfathomable red. I stood as one convicted, as a too-daring one, awe-stricken. From the place where I had slept I had not dreamed of this; no tinge on the morning twilight had suggested what the obstacle of the peak withheld. I felt pale and grey as a morning mist, insubstantial as a shadow. The grasses trembled wet at my feet. Behind me the austere mountains sat unmoved, deep in undisturbed sleep or contemplation. No bird sang, no beast moved, not even the wet trees dripped. All waited for a signal, and I waited. Death was passed—life not come. I was at the gates of the day, but had come early. . . .

I was looking westward when the world awoke, looking at the grey mountains. Suddenly it was as if they blushed. Crimson appeared in a valley and ran and spread along the cliffs and rocks and over chasms, suffusing the whole westward scene. It was the world blushing as the first kiss of the sun awakened it to a new day. And as I turned, there in the east was the hero, raising himself unaided victoriously upward. It was the sun, the hot, glorious one, uprising, glistening, burning out of a sea of scarlet, changing the blood into ruby and firing every raindrop to a diamond. Most glorious it was, seen, as it were, by one alone, and that one myself, upon a peak adding my few feet to its five thousand, and taking also that crimson reflection, that rosette or favour accorded those presented at the opening of the day. At how many town pageants had one been mocker, but here was ritual that stood majestic, imperious in its meaning—only to be revered.

The ceremony was at length over. The day was opened, the freedom of the world had been given, one had but to step down into the gardens laid open to man.

Stephen Graham

LXI: THE MYSTIC UNICORN OF THE MONTANA SUNSET

On the mountain peak, called " Going-To-The-Sun,"
I saw the Unicorn-No-Storm-Can-Tame.
The centre of the sun was but his eye,
His mane was but the sun rays and the flame.
There in that Glacier Park, above green pastures,
There above Stephen's camp fire in the rocks,
He foamed and pawed and whinnied round the world.
His feathered sides and plumes and bristling locks
Seemed but the banners of a great announcement
That unicorns were spry as heretofore,
That not a camp fire of the world was dead.
That dragons lived in them, and thousands more
Camp-born, were clawing at the clouds of Asia,
Were rising with to-morrow's dawn for men,
Camp-fire dragons, with the ancient unicorn
Bringing the Rosicrucian days again.

Any unicorn can drive away
Any thoughts the grown-up race has spoiled.
When I heard the Unicorn-of-Sunset ramping
New fancies in my veins bubbled and boiled.
Any unicorn is worth his oats,
And so we fed him bacon, and we made
An extra cup of tea, which he drank.
Then he curled up coltwise, and in slumber sank.
Dragons sprang up, next day, where he had stayed.
They were in Fujiyama silks arrayed,
Or spoke of Everest to Stephen. Then began
Discussing the strange peak in Darien
That poets climb to see the Pacific well.
How Stephen climbed it later, I will let him tell.
Following the Unicorn-No-Storm-Can-Tame
Alone, in tropic woods, is a great game.

Vachel Lindsay

LXII: IN LAPLAND

It was six o'clock before we marched off once more,
and from here on our way went for the most part
downhill. We were little the better for that. We had
already remarked a peculiarity about Svakko—uphill,
downhill, and across the level he took always the
same pace. We would have been glad of a slackening
on the uphill, but on the levels and downhill we could
have gone faster. We found, to our cost, that if we
hurried the speed on a level spot, up the next ascent
Svakko charged like a chamois, and left us to find our
own way, so for the sake of more intimate guidance,
which was really valuable across those trackless places,

we let him take his own pace, or, rather, his estimate of ours.

The descent to the Kaitumjaure hut was a résumé of what had gone before: heather-step, open moraine, covered moraine, with occasional streams or bogs, complicated by the steepness of the hillside we were traversing and by the night which was fast closing in upon us. We had now been nine hours from the tourist shelter at Kebnekaise and had walked some eighteen miles over the most uncomfortable country. Yet we were not actually tired. Now we could understand what Sarri meant when he said that the Stockholm air was too thick. This air was a tonic in itself. We grew not more tired, but fresher by the exercise: we felt after nine hours that we could go on for another nine. Physically we felt thus, but mentally we were quite weary. It was with a keen sensation of pleasure that we came down through a wood of stunted birches, and, after having made our way in the dusk for some distance between the trees, we heard Svakko cry out:

" There is our home."

On a little eminence, overlooking a lake, near a running stream was a small turf hut of Lapp pattern. I flung my rucksack at the door, shrugged my shoulders back into normal humanity, and lit a pipe. But it was darkening now. Svakko without delay foraged the birch wood for drying sticks, and cut some great armfuls of fresh birch branches for our mattress.

The fire repeated our experience at Nikhulahti. It would not burn properly but came rolling out in clouds from the door, having first filled the interior. Svakko lay on his stomach and blew it angrily without effect. At last, looking up, he found that some former traveller, obviously our herculean Finn, had quite blocked up the vent-hole with flat stones. Dislodging these we soon had a hot blaze, and content now to be roasted we crowded into the little hut, absorbing to the full that strange emotional satisfaction you may win by thrusting yourself back into a primitive state for a time.

The primitive and the modern were queerly mingled in the evening meal of Svakko. He had taken off his soft clumsy boots and had withdrawn from his legs the long leather leggings. On the march we had been struck by his mediæval appearance; with his tall bonnet, his jerkin, his broad leather belt, his swinging knife in its ivory sheath, his long leather leggings and rough boots, he was a figure appropriate enough to some fourteenth-century drawing. You might have unearthed him from Pisanello's sketch-book without incongruity. Now, his boots off, his toes warming in the blaze, he was carefully engaged in spreading before the fire to dry the grass with which his boots had been stuffed.

" Nothing like grass for walking in," he said complacently.

His evening meal began with the mangy bone of old reindeer, which he whittled, peeling the dried and rusty-looking meat away as one barks a stick. He offered a slice to us, but we had not the Lapp stomach. Then he ogled his six-pound tin of corned beef, but was faced with the problem which defeated " three men in a boat," that of opening a tin without an opener. He did not dare use his own knife upon it, for on the edge of his knife his life might depend, and if I had not carried an old and trusty hedger's blade we fear that Svakko would have carried his six pounds of corned beef all the way to Suorva and back again. This might seem absurd in an accredited guide, but there seemed to be something almost inexperienced in Svakko. We are inclined to think that he did not often make the crossing between Kebnekaise and Saltoluokta, being rather reserved for the ascent of the Kebnekaise mountain. Svakko's kettle was an old preserve tin fitted with a wire handle. In this he made his coffee, putting the coffee into cold water and bringing it up to the boil; but his cup was a Lapp wooden bowl scooped from the bole of a birch tree and curiously carved. He did not salt his coffee in Lapp fashion, but filled it with cheese parings, thus making it half coffee, half Welsh rarebit.

Then, his meal finished, he rolled himself up in the tent canvas and was asleep in a moment.

We were more leisurely in our preparations. There were reindeer skins to lay upon the ground, and in spreading one over the birch leaves for our bed, I discovered a pill box. An extra English name, the name of Beachen, Buggins & Henry, of Dartford Street, London, W., stared at me. " The mixture as before." Lord! How these firms do advertise.

Jan and Cora Gordon

LXIII

I wandered down the mountain. A little secret path, one of many, saved me the long windings of the road. It followed down the central hollow of the great cleft and accompanied the stream. All the way for miles the water tumbled in fall after fall over a hundred steps of rock, and its noise mixed with the freshness of the air, and its splashing weighted the overhanging branches of the trees. A little rain that fell from time to time through the clear morning seemed like a sister to the spray of the waterfalls; and what with all this moisture and greenery, and the surrounding silence, all the valley was inspired with content. It was a repose to descend through its leaves and grasses, and find the lovely pastures at the foot of the descent, a narrow floor between the hills. Here there were the first houses of men; and from one smoke was already going up thinly into the morning. The air was very pure and cold; it was made more nourishing and human by the presence and noise of the waters, by the shining wet grasses and the beaded leaves all through that umbrageous valley. The shreds of clouds which, high above that calm, ran swiftly in the upper air, fed it also with soft rains from time to time as fine as dew; and through those clear and momentary showers one could see the sunlight.

Hilaire Belloc

Dared and done: at last I stand upon the summit,
    Dear and True!
Singly dared and done; the climbing both of us were
    bound to do.
Petty feat and yet prodigious: every side my glance
    was bent
O'er the grandeur and the beauty lavished through the
    whole ascent.
Ledge by ledge, out broke new marvels, now minute
    and now immense:
Earth's most exquisite disclosure, heaven's own God
    in evidence!
And no berry in its hiding, no blue space in its out-
    spread,
Pleaded to escape my footstep, challenged my emerg-
    ing head,
(As I climbed or paused from climbing, now o'er-
    branched by shrub and tree,
Now built round by rock and boulder, now at just a
    turn set free,
Stationed face to face with—Nature? rather with In-
    finitude)
—No revealment of them all, as singly I my path
    pursued,
But a bitter touched its sweetness, for the thought
    stung " Even so
Both of us had loved and wondered just the same,
    five days ago! "
Five short days, sufficient hardly to entice, from out
    its den
Splintered in the slab, this pink perfection of the
    cyclamen;

Scarce enough to heal and coat with amber gum the
  sloe-tree's gash,
Bronze the clustered wilding apple, redden ripe the
  mountain-ash:
Yet of might to place between us—Oh the barrier!
  Yon Profound
Shrinks beside it, proves a pin-point: barrier this,
  without a bound!
Boundless though it be, I reach you: somehow seem
  to have you here
—Who are there. Yes, there you dwell now, plain the
  four low walls appear;
Those are vineyards they enclose from; and the little
  spire which points
—That's Collonge, henceforth your dwelling. All the
  same, howe'er disjoints
Past from present, no less certain you are here, not
  there: have dared,
Done the feat of mountain-climbing,—five days since,
  we both prepared
Daring, doing, arm in arm, if other help should haply
  fail.
For you asked, as forth we sallied to see sunset from
  the vale,
" Why not try for once the mountain,—take a fore-
  taste, snatch by stealth
Sight and sound, some unconsidered fragment of the
  hoarded wealth?
Six weeks at its base, yet never once have we together
  won
Sight or sound by honest climbing: let us two have
  dared and done
Just so much of twilight journey as may prove to-
  morrow's jaunt

127

Not the only mode of warfare—wheeled to reach the
   eagle's haunt!"
So, we turned from the low grass-path you were
   pleased to call "your own,"
Set our faces to the rose-bloom o'er the summit's
   front of stone
Where Saleve obtains, from Jura and the sunken sun
   she hides,
Due return of blushing "Good Night," rosy as a
   borne-off bride's,
For his masculine "Good Morrow" when, with sun-
   rise still in hold,
Gay he hails her, and, magnific, thrilled her black
   length burns to gold.
Up and up we went, how careless—nay, how joyous!
   All was new,
All was strange. "Call progress toilsome? that were
   just insulting you!
How the trees must temper noontide! Ah, the thicket's
   sudden break!
What will be the morning glory, when at dusk thus
   gleams the lake?
Light by light puts forth Geneva: what a land—and,
   of the land,
Can there be a lovelier station than this spot where
   now we stand?
Is it late, and wrong to linger? True, to-morrow makes
   amends.
Toilsome progress? child's play, call it—specially
   when one descends!
There, the dread descent is over—hardly our adventure, though!
Take the vale where late we left it, pace the grass-path,
   'mine,' you know!

128

Proud completion of achievement! " And we paced it,
praising still
That soft tread on velvet verdure as it wound through
hill and hill;
And at very end there met us, coming from Collonge,
the pair
—All our people of the Chalet—two, enough and none
to spare,
So, we made for home together, and we reached it as
the stars
One by one came lamping—chiefly that prepotency
of Mars—
And your last word was " I owe you this enjoyment! "
—met with " Nay:
With yourself it rests to have a month of morrows like
to-day! "
Then the meal, with talk and laughter, and the news
of that rare nook
Yet untroubled by the tourist, touched on by no
travel book.
All the same—though latent—patent, hybrid birth of
land and sea,
And (our travelled friend assured you)—if such
miracle might be—
Comparable for completeness of both blessings—all
around
Nature, and inside her circle, safety from world's
sight and sound—
Comparable to our Saisiaz. " Hold it fast and guard
it well!
Go and see and vouch for certain, then come back and
never tell
Living soul but us; and haply, prove our sky from
cloud as clear,

There may we four meet, praise fortune just as now,
    another year!"

Thus you charged him on departure: not without the
    final charge—
" Mind to-morrow's early meeting! We must leave
    our journey marge
Ample for the wayside wonders: there's the stoppage
    at the inn
Three-parts up the mountain, where the hardships of
    the track begin;
There's the convent worth a visit; but, the triumph
    crowning all—
There's Saleve's own platform facing glory which
    strikes greatness small,
—Blanc, supreme above his earth-brood, needles red
    and white and green,
Horns of silver, fangs of crystal set on edge in his
    demesne.
So, some three weeks since, we saw them: so, to-
    morrow we intend
You shall see them likewise; therefore Good Night
    till to-morrow, friend!"
Last, the nothings that extinguish embers of a vivid
    day:
" What might be the Marshal's next move, what
    Gambetta's counter-play?"
Till the landing on the staircase saw escape the latest
    spark:
" Sleep you well!" " Sleep but as well, you!"—lazy
    love quenched, all was dark.

Nothing dark next day at sundawn! Up I rose and
    forth I fared:

Took my plunge within the bath-pool, pacified the
watch-dog scared,
Saw proceed the transmutation—Jura's back to one
gold glow,
Trod your level path that let me drink the morning
deep and slow,
Reached the little quarry—ravage recompensed by
shrub and fern—
Till the overflowing ardours told me time was for return.
So, return I did, and gaily. But, for once, from no far
mound
Waved salute a tall white figure. " Has her sleep been
so profound?
Foresight, rather, prudent saving strength for day's
expenditure!
Ay, the chamber-window's open: out and on the
terrace sure! "

No, the terrace showed no figure, tall, white, leaning
through the wreaths,
Tangle-twine of leaf and bloom that intercept the air
one breathes,
Interpose between one's love and Nature's loving,
hill and dale
Down to where the blue lake's wrinkle marks the
river's inrush pale
—Mazy Arve: whereon no vessel but goes sliding
white and plain,
Not a steamboat pants from harbour but one hears
pulsate amain,
Past the city's congregated peace of homes and pomp
of spires
—Man's mild protest that there's something more
than Nature, man requires,

And that, useful as is Nature to attract the tourist's
    foot,
Quiet slow sure money-making proves the matter's
    very root,—
Need for body,—while the spirit also needs a comfort
    reached
By no help of lake or mountain, but the texts whence
    Calvin preached.
" Here's the veil withdrawn from landscape: up to
    Jura and beyond,
All awaits us ranged and ready; yet she violates the
    bond,
Neither leans nor looks nor listens: why is this? " A
    turn of eye
Took the whole sole answer, gave the undisputed
    reason " why! "

This dread way you had your summons! No pre-
    monitory touch,
As you talked and laughed ('tis told me) scarce a
    minute ere the clutch
Captured you in cold forever. Cold? nay, warm you
    were as life
When I raised you, while the others used, in pas-
    sionate poor strife,
All the means that seemed to promise any aid, and all
    in vain.
Gone you were, and I shall never see that earnest face
    again
Grow transparent, grow transfigured with the sudden
    light that leapt,
At the first word's provocation, from the heart-deeps
    where it slept.

Robert Browning

LXV: DAVIES LOSES HIS LEG

The snow was still deep and the mornings and evenings still cold when, a week after this, we reached Ottawa. This slow travelling was not at all to my liking, and I often persuaded my companion to make more haste towards Winnipeg. This he agreed to do; so the next morning we jumped a freight train, determined to hold it for the whole day. Unfortunately it was simply a local train, and being very slow, having to stop on the way at every insignificant little station, we left it, at a town called Renfrew, intending that night to beat a fast overland passenger train, which would convey us four or five hundred miles before daybreak. With this object we sat in the station's waiting room until evening, and then, some twenty minutes before the train came due, we slipped out unobserved and took possession of an empty car, stationary some distance away, from which place we could see the train coming, and yet be unseen from the station's platform. This train would soon arrive, for passengers were already pacing the platform, the luggage was placed in readiness, and a number of curious people, having nothing else to do, had assembled here to see the coming and going of the train. At last we heard its whistle, and, looking out, we saw the headlight in the distance, drawing nearer and nearer. It steamed into the station without making much noise, for the rails were slippery, there still being much ice and snow on the track. " Come," I said to Jack, " there is no time to lose "; and we quickly jumped out of the empty car.

This fast passenger train carried a blind baggage car, which means that the end nearest to the engine was blind in having no door. Our object was to suddenly appear from a hiding place, darkness being favourable, and leap on the step of this car, and from that place to the platform; this being done when the train was in motion, knowing that the conductor, who was always on the watch for such doings, rarely stopped the train to put men off, even when sure of their presence. If he saw us before the train started, he would certainly take means to prevent us from riding. When we had once taken possession of this car, no man could approach us until we reached the next stopping place, which would probably be fifty miles, or much more. At that place we would dismount, conceal ourselves, and, when it was again in motion, make another leap for our former place. Of course, the engineer and fireman could reach us, but these men were always indifferent, and never interfered, their business being ahead instead of behind the engine.

The train whistled almost before we were ready, and pulled slowly out of the station. I allowed my companion the advantage of being the first to jump, owing to his maimed hand. The train was now going faster and faster, and we were forced to keep pace with it. Making a leap he caught the handle-bar and sprang lightly on the step, after which my hand quickly took possession of this bar, and I ran with the train, prepared to follow his example. To my surprise, instead of at once taking his place on the platform, my companion stood thoughtlessly irresolute on the step, leaving me no room to make the attempt. But I still held to the bar, though the train was now going so fast that I found great difficulty in keeping step with it. I shouted to him to clear the step. This he proceeded to do, very deliberately, I thought. Taking a firmer grip on the bar, I jumped, but it was too late, for the train was now going at a rapid rate. My foot came short of the step, and I fell, and, still clinging to the handle-bar, was dragged several yards before I relinquished my hold. And there I lay for several minutes, feeling a little shaken, whilst the train passed swiftly on into the darkness.

Even then I did not know what had happened, for I attempted to stand, but found that something had happened to prevent me from doing this. Sitting down in an upright position, I then began to examine myself, and now found that the right foot was severed from the ankle. This discovery did not shock me so much as the thoughts which quickly followed. For, as I could feel no pain, I did not know but what my body was in several parts, and I was not satisfied until I had examined every portion of it. Seeing a man crossing the track, I shouted to him for assistance. He looked in one direction and another, not seeing me in the darkness, and was going his way when I shouted again. This time he looked full my way, but instead of coming nearer, he made one bound in the air, nearly fell, scrambled to his feet, and was off like the shot from a gun. This man was sought after for several weeks, by people curious to know who he was, but was never found, and no man came forward to say— " I am he." Having failed to find this man, people at last began to think I was under a ghostly impression. Probably that was the other man's impression, for who ever saw Pity make the same speed as Fear?

Another man, after this, approached, who was a workman on the line, and at the sound of my voice he seemed to understand at once what had occurred.

Coming forward quickly, he looked me over, went away, and in a minute or two returned with the assistance of several others to convey me to the station. A number of people were still there; so that when I was placed in the waiting-room to bide the arrival of a doctor, I could see no other way of keeping a calm face before such a number of eyes than by taking out my pipe and smoking, an action which, I am told, caused much sensation in the local press.

W. H. Davies

LXVI: GLORY OF THE OPEN SPACES

I have lately been passing some glorious days and nights, tramping and living with Nature in the wilds on the shores of the Murray Lakes in South Australia. It has been a time of solitude and reflection, a tuning of my soul to the wild birds' songs and the lulling wash of waves on quiet shores. Here on the shores of the Murray Lakes I have come into my own.

Forever impressed upon my mind has been the song of the harvest bird, trilled over quiet fields, reawakening, as it has, chords of happy memory. In the music of the larks I sensed anew a silent gully by Eden in Mount Lofty Hills, where I had first heard the song. Lying awake by the shore I have caught the sound of water-birds calling far away in the swamp lands, a weird and eerie medley. Gazing into the sky I have glimpsed the fleeting forms of wild duck flying across the face of the moon, whereby I saw again a lone billabong, where the moonbeams played, out on the Tallywalka, in the West Darling, where I had last seen the like. To one who had existed unwillingly long months 'mid the bricks and mortar of a big town, these sights and sounds have come like a new life, or, rather, like an old life renewed. There is oft an enhallowing beauty in remembrance.

Some days I have tramped miles of lake-shore; in others I have sauntered far out into the beautiful valley of the Finniss, or back in the lee of the blue hills among the scrubs. Each has held its endearing charms; but methinks it has been the long sweeps of lone lakeside, oft silent as the grave save for the lap of waters and the calls and whirring of water-fowl, that have allured the most. I have found in the lakes a wildness that was not in the scrubs, nor on the roads; and I, for one, have known no stronger call than the pristine. Perhaps it is that I am but few removes from the latent savage.

Every day on the open shores, carrying no gun, but coming merely as an observer and a seeker, I have watched the wild birds in the shallows seeking their food from God. I have seen that in the kingdom of the birds there exists a happy fraternity that alas! is not to be found among men. What grander sight than the wild bird carrying in his bill the food for his nesting mate and young. In a little bay down on the lakes I have watched day by day the coot, the duck, the swan, and the pelican, all feeding together like one happy brood, and for whole hours have seen no dissension. Yet at certain times and places I have known strong gourmands of men buffet the weaker and the gentler that they themselves might know no want. Truly, the wild birds teach us many lessons.

I have met with many pelican, queerest, most grotesque of birds, in my wanderings in the lake-lands. In the Albert Passage, which connects Lake

Alexandrina with Lake Albert, I came to where whole colonies of the big-pouched birds were scooping up "tookerie" from the shallows, and laughed heartily at their quaintness. The most solemn and patient of fishers, the pelican is the Izaak Walton of birdland.

And the swan—that rara avis which white settlement brought into fact—no fabled creature was ever so graceful as this. Stand at the lakeside and watch, as I have watched, at dawn and sunset, flight after flight of the grand old birds, moving in serried line over the face of the waters, and you will be richer for having seen. Twenty feet above the surface, necks craned straight before them, in swift and rushing flight they go, perfect embodiments of beauty and strength. A noble bird is the big black swan of Australia. In the air or on the water, no matter where, he looks what he is—one of God's divinest creatures.

Deep amid the tangles of a rush bed by the shore sounds the shrill, far-reaching call of a bird. Quick as thought comes the beat of feet on water, the whir of countless wings, and a covey of ducks whisk far across the lakes. 'Tis the Spur-wing Plover speeding his warning to the wilds.

Out among the gums, many of which are now bursting into bloom, I have been watching the honey-eaters executing acrobatic stunts in the foliage. See! there they are now, clinging head down to that big cluster of swaying gum blossom. With what joy and zest they have worked. All day long their brush-like tongues have been gathering in the honey from the blooms. Flowering season among the gums is clover time for the honey-eaters.

One morning, by following a willy-nilly of sounds, I surprised a family of babblers foraging amid the debris in a thicket of honeysuckle and blackboys. Such revels, such a jamboree as you never saw before. Then lo! I am seen. Instantly the babel increases twofold, surprise and indignation in every note. A hop and a flutter, and they are gone, their noisy jabbering telling the way of their going for minutes after. I was sorry to disturb them, but found humour in the scene.

It has been a pretty sight, sitting at evening by Milang, to see the swallows assembling to roost on the wooden piles of the pier. Not all of our swallows fly northward at the coming of winter. Many remain with us the whole year round. The first flight has come at sunset, two score or more, skimming and volplaning over the waters like miniature waterplanes. Down across the fields, and from the blue Mount Lofty Hills they come, more and still more, whole clouds of them, until the ethereal sphere is filled with their wee dark forms, and resonant with chirruping. Wistful of our going, how they scolded us—we humans who dared to usurp their immemorial resting place. As far back as they could remember they had known no other; in the remembrance of the most aged there had been no intrusion as this. Thus, their chirping seemed to say. At length, weary of flight, they lined the ropes and moorings of the fisher-boats, until the thin strands stood large as giant cables. It took pity at this, and came away, at which they flew like showers of darts for the piles, and by the time I had reached shore not a swallow could be seen.

I have seen no emu or kangaroo in my journeying on these lakesides. I doubt if there be one survivor. I believe the gunner has shot them out long since. The pity of it.

Day by day I have marked many changing colour schemes upon the lakes' surface. At times I have known them to be muddy-hued; at other they have been as blue as the ocean; while on one occasion I saw a silvery greyness settle down upon their face. At sunrise I have seen them a livid sheet of blood-red; at sunset I have looked out over a bale of burnished gold. So much for atmospheric effects. Actually, I knew the waters were brown with mud, minute earth-particles from snowbound Kosciusko's face and the plains of the Riverine.

The Glory of the Open Spaces. There is no life like it, this living in the clear, fresh air of the country. I think it was Thoreau who said " Truly, our greatest blessings are very cheap," and who among us will dare refute him? Sunlight, water, and the rain, the freshening winds and the air we breathe, speech, sight, love, slumber, and the starlight night—all are ours even without the asking or the praying. Do we ever give it thought? I wonder.

In my wanderings up and down these lone shores of the Murray Lakes, I have been led to gaze upon many pictures, to reflect upon many themes, to come face to face with many truths.

Sauntering one day last June along a white, lime-stone road that ran by leagues of lake-shore, I descried far ahead a large dark object that looked neither man nor beast. Moving down toward me, it drew near and passed me by. It was a duck-shooter cycling in from his hunting grounds somewhere down the lake. Slung across his back, dangling from his neck, bulging in his pockets, hanging from the fork of his cycle and from its handle-bar—everywhere about him save on the slowly revolving wheels—were the dead forms of wild duck. He was a cycling poulterer's shop. On those moonlit nights in June it often happened that I was awakened by the bursts of gunshots. Sometimes I was near enough to hear the spatter of the shot and the quack, quack of the affrighted duck. The wild bird's life is not a happy one when the gunners are in the swamps.

To-day I have been wandering along miles of open foreshore with crowds of " toorie " skedaddling in my front, and tiny sandpipers skipping at my side along the water's edge. Out upon the tops of the broken clumps and tangled skein of the fringing rushbeds many an old baldcoot has stood to watch me pass, half apprehensive of my mission. A little weary of long tramping, I lay an hour on the rippled shore of a quiet inlet, and watched some tiny bits of fluff a-bobbing up and a-bobbing down in the waters— a bob-down-you're-spotted sort of action, quaintly pretty and almost magical in its swiftness. It was a brood of grebes hunting their " daily bread." Not every dive yielded bread, or rather, with the grebes, small fry of water life. Dive after dive brought little result, until suddenly, from his forty-ninth immersion, up one comes, a squirming baby yabbie held tightly in his bill. By the grebes I have been taught patience and endeavour.

You should have seen the lakes last night, shimmering 'neath the beams of the rising moon. A weird and eerie scene forsooth, potent with silent mystery, yet beautiful withal. It was just such a night as the " wylo " loves, and I waited long to hear his cry, expecting it to rise from yonder swamp, but nothing came—the gentle lap of ebbing waters and the distant call of wildfowl alone broke the vast, moon-rayed silence. Sad, is it not, that the curlew should now be so seldom heard in a region where he was once so plentiful!

One day recently a great wind came bowling across the lakes, whereupon the waters rose in a tumult and charged shorewards in long, white-crested rollers. One marvelled that waves so high could rise upon an expanse so small, even though they did overtop and spill themselves in the shallows. With the rising of the wind, the wild birds flew for shelter, some to the backwaters on the river and others to the tall grass swamps in Albert Passage; and while the storm prevailed scarce a bird showed out along the shores. With the succeeding calm, however, they were back in hundreds, searching for tit-bits among the storm-wrack. He is a wonderful barometer, is the water-bird, and of them all none is so wondrous as the swan, which as a seer of approaching storm is almost uncanny in his wisdom.

Sunshine, a little cloud, and freshening winds that have come bowling out of a windy east have been among the many emoluments of my wanderings in lakeland. Walking out upon the bald, down-like pastures, I have drunk of a morning air almost intoxicating in its refulgency. Keen as a scimitar, yet clear as morning dew and sweet with the smell of pasture, were the dawn winds.

Tramping along the western shores, I have breathed of winds that have blown across leagues of space— wide waters and wider plains, drinking gladly of the health that was in them. What mattered if the sudden gust pummelled me with playful buffet, now from this way, now from that, or lifted and cast my hat abroad upon the meadows. If the winds have retarded my footsteps to-day, driven me back, halted me and pummelled me, to-morrow they will follow in my wake, helping me along.

The wild rhythm of the winds. With soul attuned they hold for us a finer melody than we are wont to imagine or are ready to bestow. The sounding winds are not always mere emissions of blustering howls and moans. In the winds are many songs—siren songs that fill the soul with rapture, and lulling songs that drowse the mind to rest.

The singing breezes of the open spaces. There is nothing on earth so laden with life's elixir as these. Drawing my breath from them, I have tramped long marches, whole days, sun up to sun down, and known but little weariness. For in the winds is the oldest medicine in the world, not bottled up for sale by druggist, but far-flung by the Great Alchemist, and free to all who seek it.

G. E. Archer Russell

LXVII: FROM " WALDEN "

Near the end of March, 1845, I borrowed an axe and went down to the woods by Walden Pond, nearest to where I intended to build my house, and began to cut down some tall arrowy white pines, still in their youth, for timber. It is difficult to begin without borrowing, but perhaps it is the most generous course thus to permit your fellow-men to have an interest in your enterprise. The owner of the axe, as he released his hold upon it, said that it was the apple of his eye; but I returned it sharper than I received it. It was a pleasant hillside where I worked, covered with pine woods, through which I looked out on the pond, and a small open field in the woods where pines and hickories were springing up. The ice in the pond was not yet dissolved, though there were some open spaces, and it was all dark coloured and saturated with water. There were some slight flurries of snow during the day that I worked there; but for the most part when I came out on to the railroad, on my way home, its yellow sand heap stretched away gleaming in the hazy atmosphere, and the rails shone in the spring sun, and I heard the lark and pewee and other birds already come to commence another year with us. They were pleasant spring days, in which the winter of man's discontent was thawing as well as the earth, and the life that had lain torpid began to stretch itself. One day, when my axe had come off and I had cut a green hickory for a wedge, driving it with a stone, and had placed the whole to soak in a pond hole in order to swell the wood, I saw a striped snake run into the water, and he lay on the bottom, apparently without inconvenience, as long as I staid there, or more than a quarter of an hour; perhaps because he had not yet fairly come out of the torpid state. It appeared to me that for a like reason men remain in their present low and primitive condition; but if they should feel the influence of the spring of springs arousing them, they would of necessity rise to a higher and more ethereal life. I had previously seen the snakes in frosty mornings in my path with portions of their bodies still numb and inflexible, waiting for the sun to thaw them. On the 1st of April it rained and melted the ice, and in the early part of the day, which was very foggy, I heard a stray goose groping about over the pond and cackling as if lost, or like the spirit of the fog.

So I went on for some days cutting and hewing timber, and also studs and rafters, all with my narrow axe, not having many communicable or scholar-like thoughts, singing to myself,—

> " Men say they know many things;
> But lo! they have taken wings,—
> The arts and sciences,
> And a thousand appliances;
> The wind that blows
> Is all that anybody knows."

Henry David Thoreau

LXVIII: ON THE ROAD TO ROME

I

Great men must be accustomed to have every head turned round as they pass, and to hear the whisper, " That is ——," and I have been told they consider it anything but disagreeable; but I could not lay the flattering unction to my soul that the people turned to look at the wonderful walker. When I reached my hotel at Saarbruck and looked in the glass the affair was explained. The skin was peeled or peeling off my face, and gave me a most comical appearance; and what was more, it was so sore I could not bear to touch it with cold water, and shaving was impossible.

I mention this as wishing to point out the inconveniences and even the sufferings of a walking-tour. Besides the skin of my face, my ears from constant exposure were so sore at times that I could not lie on either side in bed. Then every one of my ten toes seemed determined to remind me of its existence. When the toes ceased the heels began. Still these were mere *bagatelles* compared to the splendid health I was otherwise enjoying; spots on the sun, thorns on the rose. How I ate and slept and revelled in rude health! What an appetite I had, to be sure! I had no need to look down the bill of fare; whatever came was sure to be right. I was positively ashamed as the waiters took away nothing but empty dishes from the tables where I dined. Sometimes I put back a bone or bit of gristle for appearance' sake! At bedtime, mattress or feather bed, beds too short or beds too narrow, never for a moment disturbed my repose. I curled myself up somehow, and slept the sleep of the just. I could lie on damp grass and never get rheumatism, or sit under open windows and never have the tic. These things must be remembered in connection with the fact that I am no hardened traveller, with the stomach of an ostrich and the skin of a rhinoceros. Ever since I was fifteen I have had to earn my bread by some sedentary occupation, and have been no stranger to the ills which beset a studious life. But in the life I was living, I solved the mystery of the Wandering Jew, for I felt if I could only keep on walking, there was no reason why I should not be found promenading round the world a hundred years hence as well as I am to-day.

I I

As I pursued my road I met a tramp, and again the merry disposition of these Germans forced itself upon me. In England the moucher is a filthy, broken-spirited creature, without a particle of brightness to enliven his life. This German tramp, when I had given him a copper or two, wanted to stand me a drink, and actually proffered me a cigar! If one had to say what makes the difference between the tramps of the two countries, something must be put down to climate. Mr. Froude says the assured brightness of the climate has changed the dispositions of the Australians. In England, whatever may have been proposed—a picnic, or a week at the seaside, or a country visit—at once the mind is tormented with a fear lest all should be spoilt by the wet. If this be so with well-to-do people, what must the tramp feel?

Thoughts like these occupied many mornings. Probably many have wondered what I did think about on these lonely tramps, and what my mind worked on. Well, as a priest of the Church of England, I had my office to say morning and evening, and this took about half an hour. Then I carried a pocket *Horace* about with me, and learned many of the odes off by heart. When Byron was in Venice he wrote to a friend saying he wanted something craggy for his mind to break upon, and so he learned the Armenian language. I am not a Byron, so a few of Horace's odes and some of Monckton Milnes' poems were craggy enough for me. After that, I used to compose letters home describing my travels, and generally carried a local newspaper in my pocket that I might spell out the news as I toiled up a hill, or when for any reason I was compelled to walk slowly. But it must not be thought I was always working my mind in some way or another. Many an hour was passed in pure enjoyment of the life I was living. When George Borrow asked one of his gipsies what enjoyment he had, seeing he had no religious belief, and nothing to look forward to, the gipsy replied:

" There's the wind on the heath, master."

He referred to the enjoyment of sniffing in the keen air of the open plain, an enjoyment which railways have deprived nine-tenths of the population of knowing anything about, but which at least I and the gipsies can appreciate.

III

And now the day came when I was to enter Rome. I could scarcely sleep the night before, partly because I was so close to the stable that every time a horse kicked it woke me, and partly because the excitement would not let me sleep. I was off on my last course soon after five, with nearly thirty miles before me; and about eight, on ascending a hill, I beheld the dome of St. Peter's. I saw nothing else—no city, no building to bear up the dome, but there it was, like Mahomet's coffin, suspended between heaven and earth. I felt something like the Crusaders are said to have done when they came in sight of Jerusalem— quite overwhelmed at beholding the end and crown of all their labours. I felt a great gulp in my throat, and if there had been any one to speak to me I should have found it difficult to answer. However, I lost the dome as I descended the hill, and saw nothing more till the whole city burst upon my view. I turned into a garden to get some bread and wine, and again hastened on, quite feverish to reach my journey's end, and, as the clocks were striking twelve, I entered Rome by the Portese Gate.

A. N. Cooper
(The Walking Parson)

LXIX: FOOTPATHS

The reason for preserving to the nation the ancient bridle-paths, driftways, and footways will not be questioned by those who consider that with each year the number of people increases who need them for their convenience, their health, and their enjoyment. The appreciation of the country walk and field-side ramble grows each year, too, with education, and with a national love for the beauty of nature and pursuit of natural history and science. Each year the nation's eyes are being so trained as to need the country more for its further education and its more intelligent pleasures. The love of scenery in the English masses is at present but semi-educated; but no one lives in a place haunted by tourists, and at times overrun with the intelligent class of artisans, but can dare to prophesy that it will yet become a passion with the people.

Canon Rawnsley

LXX: THE END OF THE ROAD

IN THESE BOOTS AND WITH THIS STAFF
Two hundred leaguers and a half
Walked I, went I, paced I, tripped I,
Marched I, held I, skelped I, slipped I,
Pushed I, panted, swung and dashed I;
Picked I, forded, swam and splashed I,
Strolled I, climbed I, crawled and scrambled,
Dropped and dipped I, ranged and rambled;
Plodded I, hobbled I, trudged and tramped I,
And in lonely spinnies camped I,
And in haunted pinewoods slept I,

Lingered, loitered, limped and crept I,
Clambered, halted, stepped and leapt I,
Slowly sauntered, roundly strode I,
And . . . .
Let me not conceal it . . . *rode* I.
(For who but critics could complain
Of " riding " in a railway train?)
Across the valley and the high-land,
With all the world on either hand,
Drinking when I had a mind to,
Singing when I felt inclined to;
Nor ever turned my face to home
Till I had slaked my heart at Rome.

Hilaire Belloc

LXXI: FROM LARISSA

Towards sunset, following the young archæologist's express recommendation, we went up to a little café on a sort of acropolis just above the river Peneus, and there beheld, in one gasp, the vision of absolute beauty we had travelled so far to seek. At our feet the river; a few miles off, as it seemed, the snowy summits of Olympus, Ossa and Pelion; between these and us a plain covered with shrubs and grass of a colour new to us, so young, so vivid, and yet so soft was the green. But the amazing thing was a middle-distance range on the right that appeared to rise suddenly out of the plain, only in Greece the light plays strange tricks. These intensely pink mountains, with cold-blue, cavernous shadows that reminded one of the mountains in the moon as seen through a powerful telescope, might have been cut out of cardboard, so sharp was the outline. In all our forty days' pilgrimage we saw nothing more ravishing than that scene: the brown and silver river, the salad-green plain, the terrifying pink cardboard range, and, behind all, those mountains of the sonorous, intoxicating names.

Ethel Smyth

LXXII: STANLEY FINDS LIVINGSTONE

As I advanced towards him I noticed he was pale, looked wearied. . . . I would have run to him, only I was a coward in the presence of such a mob—would have embraced him, only, he being an Englishman, I did not know how he would receive me.

" Dr. Livingstone, I presume? "

" Yes."

" I thank God, Doctor, I have been permitted to see you."

" I feel thankful that I am here to welcome you."

H. M. Stanley

LXXIII: CLIMBING A PEAK IN DARIEN

We made but slow progress in the jungle. Rainy weather and consequent mud held us. I changed my guide three times. None cared to go far from home. Two nights were spent in the scantiest shelter. Thousands of flaming fireflies lit the floating mists which along the edge of a jungle clearing looked like phantoms living in dark houses. The wraiths were of unstable dimensions, now swelling to a bank of mist, now tailing away to nothingness. But the fireflies lighted their way—myriads of fireflies. I lay in all the clothes I possessed and in my boots and wearing gloves, but still the mosquitoes bit. How combat a foe that you actually take in with your breath!

Tongues of fire among white mists in intense darkness, howling of monkeys, the creaking and wailing and prolonged noise of insects in the trees, mosquitoes as noiseless and attentive as breath, the air not vital, suffocating—of such were the nights. In a hotel you would turn and turn, but something in the jungle constrains you to lie like one dead all the night long, and that something also banishes thought.

There breaks out the throb of a native drum, one only, but you cannot say where it comes from. It is far away, it is close at your ear—it is wandering in the jungle. Who could be beating it, and why? But it is no matter. Your eyes close. You fall into a light slumber and lie dreamlessly—you cannot estimate how long. But suddenly horror breaks upon your soul. You start up; you look around; you fall back in a cold sweat. A roaring as of lions has torn through your consciousness. You think a puma has found you, and then, as suddenly, you laugh and relax. It is a pack of night-howling monkeys, beating their hairy breasts high among the branches and howling like lost souls. A vague thought enters the mind, the lost souls of those who murdered Indians for their gold. . . .

Morning comes and proves that each bad night was but a bad dream, a nightmare, and not God's creation. For even over the " white man's grave " it is fresh, with fair rose colours in the sky. . . .

I found that in the native huts I never had to pay for hospitality. It is true, however, that whole families enjoyed my provisions—gloated over tinned milk, drank mug after mug of dense Nombre de Dios coffee, ate chocolate as a wonderful novelty. In return, they would put in the midst of the red mud floor a large pot of rice and pieces of smoked fish and forest berries soaked in brine. They brought down branches of fat little cream-coloured bananas from the roof. A parrot would lift itself by its beak on to my fingers whilst I ate, and in the same way up my coat to my shoulder, calling and out-calling its mate who was perched on an ox-limbed woman in coloured overalls. In such a hut I met Martinez, a man with no arms and only one eye. He had lost his members dynamiting fish. Martinez had hooks tightly corded to the stumps of his wrists, and had learned to do all that most of us can do with hands—thus, he struck a match and lighted a cigarette, he shouldered my knapsack, he lifted down an old gun from the wall, he slung it on his back. Even using hooks for hands he was a good shot with a gun.

Martinez was by temperament a hunter, and was less interested in getting me to the Pacific coast than in following trails of wild beasts. He showed me a tree-sloth, hanging in the hammock of its own body high up among the branches; showed me a boa coiled like a cable and sleeping like a babe. That did not interest him. But the jaguar and the puma were ever in his thoughts. We came upon the footprints of a tiger, a *grande gato*, a perfect six-spot in the mud. With bent back and staring eye Martinez was for following it—and he gave me his long knife. But I said " No."

" No carey? " he inquired, raising his brows. " No quiere? "

" No, Martinez; *grande gato* make nice meal you

and me. Sabe, Martinez? " I made signs to him, pointing down my throat.

" Ah, you no carey? " he rejoined sadly, and set his face toward the sun. He threaded his way to an isolated hut surrounded by bog, where lived a bachelor acquaintance more ready to follow up the trail of the tiger. There we brewed coffee, and as I sat in the doorway sipping it I saw fly past like a flame the most beautiful bird I had seen in the jungle. The sportsmen missed it, but heavy as I was with clinging mud I started up to follow it. I was tired enough of tramping, wet to the waist, mud to the knees. I had fallen down several times. Armless Martinez had offered to carry me across one or two morasses and torrents, and had actually raised me on his shoulders once, but I felt him waver under me and took my two hundred pounds down from his back. I was glad when we came once more upon a stretch of the *Camino Real* and could actually walk upon it. We stepped steadily upward, and I began to meditate climbing that " goodlie and high tree," for there were many such starting out of the marsh and the scrub and going straight to heaven. But then, suddenly and unexpectedly, coming out on the scarp of a commanding ridge, I saw the ocean. I did not need to climb a tree. From this ridge I also saw the Pacific, for the first time, far away, a blue triangle of water beyond the hills and the forests and the ridges. There was a wide and majestic view, and the great trees of the jungle made a framework on either hand like the extended plumage of an eagle.

Stephen Graham

Shakro continued for some time, describing in detail the attractions of the new life he was going to arrange for me in his home in Tiflis.

And as he talked I mused on the great unhappiness of men equipped with new morality and new aspirations—they tread the paths of life lonely and astray; and the fellow-travellers they meet on the way are alien to them, unable to understand them. Life is a heavy burden for these lonely souls. Helplessly they drift hither and thither. They are like the good seed, wafted in the air, and dropping but rarely on to fruitful soil.

Daylight had broken. The sea far away shone with rosy gold.

" I am sleepy," said Shakro.

We halted. He lay down in a trench, which the fierce gusts of wind had dug out in the dry sand, near the shore. He wrapped himself, head and all, in the overcoat, and was soon sound asleep. I sat beside him, gazing dreamily over the sea.

It was living its vast life, full of mighty movement.

The flocks of waves broke noisily on the shore and rippled over the sand, that faintly hissed as it soaked up the water. The foremost waves, crested with white foam, flung themselves with a loud boom on the shore, and retreated, driven back to meet the waves that were pushing forwards to support them. Intermingling in the foam and spray, they rolled once more towards the shore, and beat upon it, struggling to enlarge the bounds of their realm. From the horizon to the shore, across the whole expanse of waters, these supple, mighty waves rose up, moving, ever moving, in a compact mass, bound together by the oneness of their aim. The sun shone more and more brightly on the crests of the breakers, which, in the distance on the horizon, looked blood-red. Not a drop went astray in the titanic heavings of the watery mass, impelled, it seemed, by some conscious aim, which it would soon attain by its vast rhythmic blows. Enchanting was the bold beauty of the foremost waves, as they dashed stubbornly upon the silent shore, and fine it was to see the whole sea, calm and united, the mighty sea, pressing on and ever on. The sea glittered now with all the colours of the rainbow, and seemed to take a proud, conscious delight in its own power and beauty.

A large steamer glided quietly round a point of land, cleaving the waters. Swaying majestically over the troubled sea, it dashed aside the threatening crests of the waves. At any other time this splendid, strong, flashing steamer would have set me thinking of the creative genius of man, who could thus enslave the elements. But now, beside me, lay an untamed element in the shape of a man.

Maxim Gorky

LXXV: THE ULTIMATE NIGHT

You know the groan that a wheel makes when the spokes get loose and the sheaves rub against one another. I heard this sound in Old Castile, on New Year's Eve. I went down a dark street, and there by the light of the moon I found a man with a still bleeding goat's bladder stretched tight over a tin can, and he was pushing a stick in it. Every time he pushed in the stick the thing groaned. The man had a white and black serapi wrapped round his neck, an ancient Balaclava helmet on his head, sandals made from American motor tyres, and a suit of mud-stained corduroys. When I came up he grinned. And when he opened his mouth I saw that he also had two teeth.

This was New Year's Eve in Castile and I joined myself to the procession. There were two peasant women with him and a husky young girl who had a tin tambourine. There were two other men with kettles tied on their stomachs which they were using for drums, and there was a curly-haired boy playing a purple flute. The man with the groaning goat bladder walked in their lead in the shape of the letter S. His knees were bent forward, but his shoulders were bent back, so that he went down the street leaning backward all the time—and his head was lying on his chest.

O-ungh O-ungh O-ungh . . . twee-twee-tweedle-deooo . . . bangkadango. . . .

With a bent Bacchus at the van and Pan on our flank we passed down the street. I was ready for anything. I wanted to buy a sausage and hit someone with it. At four o'clock in the morning I had been in the Café des Artistes in Bilbao—but that, thank the Lord, was a couple of hundred miles away—and all day I had been coming down into the barren plains of Old Castile. They lie like the skin of a baked apple in the blue, pink and purple sierras of Spain, and on them lies Burgos, and I was in Burgos, and there wasn't another train out until eleven o'clock the next day. And I had been brooding silently in my room— thinking of other New Year's Eves I had known at the Blackstone or the Drake. You want to be in your own country when New Year rolls around. I was ready for anything—I would buy a long sausage like a sword and slay a Guardia Municipal.

" Vino! " cried Bacchus as we passed a café.

" Vino! " I sang with the chorus.

But they would not let me pay for it. We were in the café. It was fifteen feet square, seven feet high, filled with Spaniards and smoke. Some of the Spaniards were peasants, some were soldiers, and there were two officers from an African regiment with red fezzes on their smooth heads. There was a man in there with a clock-face strapped on his chest. The clock was two feet broad, and after every drink he cocked his head over its edge and shoved it on one minute.

" Vino! " he shrieked.

By his clock the time was twenty minutes to twelve. But he was five minutes late. I showed him my wrist watch. And he corrected it.

Fifteen minutes before the New Year.

The young girl whirled before me and banged her tin tambourine. Bacchus groaned with his bladder. The Castilians drummed on their kettles. And we marched out for the Plaza Mayor.

" Vino! " shouted Bacchus as we passed a café.

158

I said it was my turn this time, and we lined up for drinks. Bacchus wanted a cognac, he said. The rest of us drank pink wine, which had been watered for the occasion. The men and girls behind the bar shot them across to us like quoits. The man with the clock shoved it on twenty minutes—and I put it back.

Ten minutes before the New Year.

Bacchus tried to kiss me, but I told him not this year. In this café we were joined by the Lilliputian Brigade. These were small Castilians of high school age. Their heads just reached my shoulder. " Vino! " they shouted, and " Vino! " I replied. But they would not let me pay for it. The proudest Castilian of the hot blood of Spain, a Castilian in black beret and pale brown velveteen, produced a peseta and paid for the lot of us.

The Lilliputians were all playing purple flutes.

There was a high hooded cart standing before this café, and its train of four weary mules. The mules were leaning forward with their ears down their noses. The Lilliputians tried to run away with them, but Bacchus and I intervened.

As we were untangling the mules from the Lilliputians two peasants came up who had entangled themselves. They were intertwined like the design of a trellised gate. Arms and legs and torsos intermingling with a leafy vine. It was tied securely around their necks. And they looked out from this at us, pushing aside their verdure, and invited us to come inside and have a drink. They and their arbour joined our parade.

Tweedlede-ooooo went the Lilliputian brigade.

At 12 o'clock, in the Plaza Mayor, you are supposed to eat twelve grapes. This brings you happiness for the New Year. You eat them quickly, one with each stroke of the clock. And we marched there now to secure our supply. The peasants were selling them in little lighted carts around the arcades. And I saw now where the vine-leafed gentlemen had got their design. They had removed one of the long wreaths from the top of a cart. We bought twelve grapes each, wrapped up in little cornucopias of white paper.

The Plaza Mayor is a pentagon of stone around an oval of small pines. It is shaped like a tennis racket, paved with hexagonal blocks. The peasants were dancing on these. They danced in circles, holding each other's hands. They danced in pairs. They danced in lines of eight girls abreast—their black hair flinging up against the moon. They danced around an old Castilian holding up an open umbrella. They danced with peasants on each other's backs. They danced to flutes, they danced to drums—they danced to the twang of guitars.

" Vino! " squeaked the Lilliputian brigade.

They led me off to a café through the yellow stone walls of the arcade. They romped about me under the dirty lights and pulled at my trench-coat. " Vino! " they piped.

But I was looking through the smoke. The two African officers were standing by the bar with two girls. The girls were taller than they. Two tall girls with yellow hair and blue eyes. They were staring at me—they stared.

" English," squeaked one of the Lilliputians, pointing at them.

The girls spoke to their officers and went out. I gave them some time and then I went too. The Lilliputians gambolled after me. As we stepped from the arcades a rocket went up. It exploded in the sky. I heard the first stroke of the bell. Another rocket went up and exploded overhead.

I was eating my grapes—to bring me good luck. At each stroke of the bell I put in a grape. I had eaten eleven of them and then I looked at the girl. She was standing beside me, with the grinning African officer's arm around her waist. We looked at each other as we ate the last grape.

" Happy New Year," I said.

" Thanks."

I looked at the man with the clock. It had lost both its hands.

Negley Farson

LXXVI

When first they saw the men of Rome walking for
the pleasure of walking, they thought they must be
mad.

Strabo III, 164

LXXVII: KANSAS

Oh, I have walked in Kansas
Through many a harvest field
And piled the sheaves of glory there
And down the wild rows reeled:

Each sheaf a little yellow sun,
A heap of hot-rayed gold;
Each binder like Creation's hand
To mould suns, as of old.

Straight overhead the orb of noon
Beat down with brimstone breath;
The desert wind from south and west
Was blistering flame and death.

Yet it was gay in Kansas,
A-fighting that strong sun;
And I and many a fellow-tramp
Defied that wind and won.

And we felt free in Kansas
From any sort of fear,
For thirty thousand tramps like us
There harvest every year.

She stretches arms for them to come,
She roars for helpers then,
And so it is in Kansas
That tramps, one month, are men.

We sang in burning Kansas
The songs of Sabbath-school,
The " Day Star " flashing in the East,
The " Vale of Eden " cool.

We sang in splendid Kansas
" The flag that set us free "—
That march of fifty thousand men
With Sherman to the sea.

We feasted high in Kansas
And had much milk and meat.
The tables groaned to give us power
Wherewith to save the wheat.

Our beds were sweet alfalfa hay
Within the barn-loft wide.
The loft-doors opened out upon
The endless wheat-field tide.

I loved to watch the windmills spin
And watch that big moon rise,
I dreamed and dreamed with lids half shut,
The moonlight in my eyes.

For all men dream in Kansas
By noonday and by night,
By sunrise yellow, red and wild,
And moonrise wild and white.

The wind would drive the glittering clouds,
The cottonwoods would croon,
And past the sheaves and through the leaves
Came whispers from the moon.

Vachel Lindsay

LXXVIII: THE LEECH GATHERER

There was a roaring in the wind all night;
The rain came heavily and fell in floods;
But now the sun is rising calm and bright;
The birds are singing in the distant woods;
Over his own sweet voice the stock-dove broods;
The jay makes answer as the magpie chatters;
And all the air is filled with pleasant noise of waters.

All things that love the sun are out of doors;
The sky rejoices in the morning's birth;
The grass is bright with raindrops;—on the moors
The hare is running races in her mirth;
And with her feet she from the plashy earth
Raises a mist that, glittering in the sun,
Runs with her all the way, wherever she doth run.

I was a traveller then upon the moor;
I saw the hare that raced about with joy;
I heard the woods, the distant waters, roar,
Or heard them not, as happy as a boy;
The pleasant season did my heart employ;
My old remembrances went from me wholly;
And all the ways of men so vain and melancholy!

But, as it sometimes chanceth, from the might
Of joy in minds that can no further go,
As high as we have mounted in delight
In our dejection do we sink as low.
To me that morning did it happen so;
And fears, and fancies, thick upon me came;
Dim sadness—and blind thoughts, I know not, nor
    could name.

I heard the skylark warbling in the sky;
And I bethought me of the playful hare;
Even such a happy child of earth am I;
Even as these blissful creatures do I fare;
Far from the world I walk, and from all care;
But there may come another day to me—
Solitude, pain of heart, distress, and poverty?

My whole life I have lived in pleasant thought,
As if life's business were a summer mood;
As if all needful things would come unsought
To genial faith, still rich in genial good;
But how can he expect that others should
Build for him, sow for him, and at his call
Love him, who for himself will take no heed at all?

I thought of Chatterton, the marvellous boy,
The sleepless soul that perished in his pride;
Of him who walked in glory and in joy
Following his plough, along the mountain-side;
By our own spirits are we deified:
We poets in our youth begin in gladness;
But thereof comes in the end despondency and mad-
    ness.

Now, whether it were by peculiar grace,
A leading from above, a something given,
Yet it befell, that, in this lonely place,
When I with these untoward thoughts had striven,
Beside a pool bare to the eye of heaven
I saw a man before me unawares;
The oldest man he seemed that ever wore grey hairs.

As a huge stone is sometimes seen to lie
Couched on the bald top of an eminence;
Wonder to all who do the same espy,
By what means it could thither come, and whence;
So that it seems a thing endued with sense;
Like a sea-beast crawled forth, that on a shelf
Of rock or sand reposeth, there to sun itself;

Such seemed this man, not all alive nor dead,
Nor all asleep—in his extreme old age;
His body was bent double, feet and head
Coming together in life's pilgrimage;
As if some dire constraint of pain, or rage
Of sickness felt by him in times long past,
A more than human weight upon his frame had cast.

Himself he propped, his body, limbs, and face,
Upon a long grey staff of shaven wood:
And, still as I drew near with gentle pace,
Upon the margin of that moorish flood
Motionless as a cloud the old man stood;
That heareth not the loud winds when they call;
And moveth altogether, if it move at all.

At length, himself unsettling, he the pond
Stirred with his staff, and fixedly did look

Upon the muddy waters, which he conned,
As if he had been reading in a book:
And now a stranger's privilege I took;
And, drawing to his side, to him did say,
" This morning gives us promise of a glorious day."

A gentle answer did the old man make,
In courteous speech which forth he slowly drew:
And him with further words I thus bespake,
" What occupation do you there pursue?
This is a lonesome place for one like you."
He answered, while a flash of mild surprise
Broke from the sable orbs of his yet vivid eyes.

His words came feebly, from a feeble chest,
But each in solemn order followed each,
With something of a lofty utterance drest;
Choice word, and measured phrase, above the reach
Of ordinary men; a stately speech;
Such as grave livers do in Scotland use,
Religious men, who give to God and man their dues.

He told, that to these waters he had come
To gather leeches, being old and poor:
Employment hazardous and wearisome!
And he had many hardships to endure:
From pond to pond he roamed, from moor to moor;
Housing, by God's good help, by choice or chance;
And in this way he gained an honest sustenance.

The old man still stood talking by my side;
But now his voice to me was like a stream
Scarce heard; nor word from word could I divide;

And the whole body of the man did seem
Like one whom I had met with in a dream;
Or like a man from some far region sent,
To give me human strength, by apt admonishment.

My former thoughts returned: the fear that kills;
And hope that is unwilling to be fed;
Cold, pain, and labour, and all fleshly ills;
And mighty poets in their misery dead.
Perplexed, and longing to be comforted
My question eagerly did I renew,
" How is that you live, and what is it you do ? "

He with a smile did then his words repeat:
And said, that, gathering leeches, far and wide
He travelled; stirring thus about his feet
The waters of the pools where they abide.
" Once I could meet with them on every side;
But they have dwindled long by slow decay;
Yet still I persevere, and find them where I may."

While he was talking thus, the lonely place,
The old man's shape, and speech, all troubled me:
In my mind's eye I seemed to see him pace
About the weary moors continually,
Wandering about alone and silently.
While I these thoughts within myself pursued,
He, having made a pause, the same discourse renewed.

And soon with this he other matter blended,
Cheerfully uttered, with demeanour kind,
But stately in the main; and when he ended,

I could have laughed myself to scorn to find
In that decrepit man so firm a mind.
" God," said I, " be my help and stay secure;
I'll think of the leech-gatherer on the lonely moor! "

William Wordsworth

LXXIX: FROM AN OUTPOST

I've tramped South England up and down
   Down Dorset way, down Devon way,
Through every little ancient town
   Down Dorset way, down Devon way.
I mind the old stone churches there,
The taverns round the market square,
The cobbled streets, the garden flowers,
The sundials telling peaceful hours
   Down Dorset way, down Devon way.

The meadowlands are green and fair
   Down Somerset and Sussex way.
The clover scent is in the air
   Down Somerset and Sussex way.
I mind the deep-thatched homesteads there,
The noble downlands, clean and bare,
The blue wood-smoke from shepherds' fires
   Down Dorset way, down Devon way.

Mayhap I shall not walk again
   Down Dorset way, down Devon way.
Nor pick a posy in a lane
   Down Somerset and Sussex way.

But though my bones, unshriven, rot
In some far-distant alien spot,
What soul I have shall rest from care
To know that meadows still are fair
　　Down Dorset way, down Devon way.

Leslie Coulson

LXXX

Ah God! to see the branches stir
Across the moon at Grantchester!
To smell the thrilling-sweet and rotten
Unforgettable, unforgotten
River-smell, and hear the breeze
Sobbing in the little trees.
Say, do the elm-clumps greatly stand
Still guardians of that holy land?
The chestnuts shade, in reverend dream,
The yet unacademic stream?
Is dawn a secret shy and cold
Anadyomene, silver-gold?
And sunset still a golden sea
From Haslingfield to Madingley?

And after, ere the night is born,
Do hares come out about the corn?
Oh, is the water sweet and cool,
Gentle and brown, above the pool?
And laughs the immortal river still
Under the mill, under the mill?

Say, is there Beauty yet to find?
And Certainty? and Quiet kind?
Deep meadows yet, for to forget
The lies, and truths, and pain? . . . oh! yet
Stands the Church clock at ten to three?
And is there honey still for tea?

Rupert Brooke

LXXXI: FROM " THE SCHOLAR GIPSY"

Here, where the reaper was at work of late—
   In this high field's dark corner, where he leaves
   His coat, his basket, and his earthen cruse,
   And in the sun all morning binds the sheaves,
      Then here, at noon, comes back his stores to use—
         Here will I sit and wait,
   While to my ear from uplands far away
      The bleating of the folded flocks is borne,
      With distant cries of reapers in the corn—
   All the live murmur of a summer's day.

Screen'd is this nook o'er the high, half-reap'd field,
   And here till sundown, shepherd! will I be.
      Through the thick corn the scarlet poppies peep,
   And round green roots and yellowing stalks I see
      Pale pink convolvulus in tendrils creep;
         And air-swept lindens yield
   Their scent, and rustle down their perfumed showers
      Of bloom on the bent grass where I am laid,
      And bower me from the August sun with shade;
   And the eye travels down to Oxford's towers.

And near me on the grass lies Glanvil's book—
  Come, let me read the oft-read tale again!
  The story of the Oxford scholar poor,
Of pregnant parts and quick inventive brain,
  Who, tired of knocking at preferment's door,
    One summer morn forsook
His friends, and went to learn the gipsy-lore,
  And roam'd the world with that wild brotherhood,
  And came, as most men deem'd, to little good,
But came to Oxford and his friends no more.

But once, years after, in the country lanes,
  Two scholars, whom at college erst he knew,
  Met him, and of his way of life enquired;
Whereat he answer'd, that the gipsy-crew,
  His mates, had arts to rule as they desired
    The workings of men's brains,
And they can bind them to what thoughts they will.
  "And I," he said, " the secret of their art,
  When fully learn'd, will to the world impart;
But it needs heaven-sent moments for this skill."

This said, he left them, and return'd no more—
  But rumours hung about the country-side,
  That the lost scholar long was seen to stray,
Seen by rare glimpses, pensive and tongue-tied,
  In hat of antique shape, and cloak of grey,
    The same the gipsies wore.
Shepherds had met him on the Hurst in spring;
  At some lone alehouse in the Berkshire moors,
  On the warm ingle-bench, the smock-frock'd
    boors
Had found him seated at their entering.

But, 'mid their drink and clatter, he would fly.
    And I myself seem half to know thy looks,
        And put the shepherds, wanderer! on thy trace;
    And boys who in lone wheatfields scare the rooks
        I ask if thou hast pass'd their quiet place;
           Or in my boat I lie
    Moor'd to the cool bank in the summer-heats,
        'Mid wide grass meadows which the sunshine fills
        And watch the warm, green-muffled Cumner hills,
    And wonder if thou haunt'st their shy retreats.

For most, I know, thou lov'st retired ground!
    Thee at the ferry Oxford riders blithe,
        Returning home on summer nights, have met
    Crossing the stripling Thames at Bab-lock-hithe,
        Trailing in the cool stream thy fingers wet,
           As the punt's rope chops round;
    And leaning backward in a pensive dream,
        And fostering in thy lap a heap of flowers
        Pluck'd in shy fields and distant Wychwood
        bowers,
    And thine eyes resting on the moonlit stream.

And then they land, and thou art seen no more!—
    Maidens, who from the distant hamlets come
        To dance around the Fyfield elm in May,
    Oft through the darkening fields have seen thee
        roam,
        Or cross a stile into the public way.
           Oft thou hast given them store
    Of flowers—the frail-leaf'd, white anemony,
        Dark bluebells drench'd with dews of summer eves,
        And purple orchises with spotted leaves—
    But none hath words she can report of thee.

And, above Godstow Bridge, when hay-time's here
    In June, and many a scythe in sunshine flames,
        Men who through those wide fields of breezy grass
    Where black-wing'd swallows haunt the glittering
            Thames,
        To bathe in the abandon'd lasher pass
            Have often pass'd thee near
    Sitting upon the river bank o'ergrown;
        Mark'd thine outlandish garb, thy figure spare,
        Thy dark vague eyes, and soft abstracted air—
    But, when they came from bathing, thou wast gone!

At some lone homestead in the Cumner hills,
    Where at her open door the housewife darns,
        Thou hast been seen, or hanging on a gate
    To watch the threshers in the mossy barns.
        Children, who early range these slopes and late
            For cresses from the rills,
    Have known thee eyeing, all an April-day,
        The springing pastures and the feeding kine;
        And mark'd thee, when the stars come out and
            shine,
    Through the long dewy grass move slow away.

In autumn, on the skirts of Bagley Wood
    Where most the gipsies by the turf-edged way
        Pitch their smoked tents, and every bush you see
    With scarlet patches tagg'd and shreds of grey,
        Above the forest-ground called Thessaly—
            The blackbird, picking food,
    Sees thee, nor stops his meal, nor fears at all;
        So often has he known thee past him stray,
        Rapt, twirling in thy hand a wither'd spray,
    And waiting for the spark from heaven to fall.

And once, in winter, on the causeway chill
    Where home through flooded fields foot travellers
        go,
    Have I not pass'd thee on the wooden bridge,
    Wrapt in thy cloak and battling with the snow,
        Thy face tow'rd Hinksey and its wintry ridge?
            And thou hast climb'd the hill,
    And gain'd the white brow of the Cumner range;
        Turn'd once to watch, while thick the snowflakes
            fall,
    The line of festal light in Christ-Church hall—
    Then sought thy straw in some sequester'd grange.
                                            Matthew Arnold

LXXXII

The open air!
Is there anything so grand and fine and beautiful
as the open air? How glorious it is to go along to no
place in particular, neither thinking of nor caring for
the morrow! Despite what fools—who are sometimes
called wise men—may say, man gets more out of life
when he lets to-morrow take care of itself. I never was
so happy in all my life as I was in the old days of
wandering along. Security! Man, when he is in a
healthy state, cares absolutely nothing for it. Security
is at best but a cowardly word. I know men who are
" secure." I know men who have plenty of money.
And, taking it all round, they don't get as much out
of life as those who live from hand to mouth.

To walk along in the glorious sunshine. How wonderful it is! How bracing it is to go along in the keen
and healthful cold! To work one's way through the

storm! It brings to the body power and strength.
There is beauty even in the fall of the rain.

How wonderful is the open air!

Bart Kennedy

LXXXIII: UP ALONG AND DOWN ALONG

When I lived up in Town I took
Delight in life as in a book
Wherein I read with mirth and grief
Things strange and passing all belief;
And so in that quick air, like flowers
Summoned from winter sleep, my powers
Awoke and, waking, found the joy
Of deepening aim and high employ,
That time, it seemed, would never avail
The rich delight of life to stale.
And yet for all—in spite of, too,
The beckoning shapes that men pursue
There nearer seen and offering them
The touch, almost, of garment hem—
At length with vague unrest I felt
That strange in a strange world I dwelt
From out whose noise and rush my heart
Would steal away and dream apart.
Soon, then, beneath the city's roar
I heard the summons of the moor,
And up the Fleet and down the Strand
The whispered call of my own land,
While so did sense of sky and steep
Possess me waking and asleep
That oft in secret I would fare
To Paddington and sadly there

N

Watch the great trains go out that glide
From London Town to Plymouth Tide.

   .   .   .   .   .

Now when I will I seek the moor,
A rough steep mile from my own door,
Where little is heard from dawn to dark
But singing of a sky-lost lark,
Or brawl of brooks in pathless combes
Like children playing in empty rooms;
While westward down the heavens the slow
Cloud ships of war a-sailing go
Above the slopes ablaze with gorse,
Till on beyond the purpling tors,
Brought-to at eve with sails close-furled,
Their snow-white fleets blockade the world.
Or else I trace the lanes that wind
Their way to places out of mind,
So deep and dark that but a thread
Of cloud-barred sky is seen o'erhead
(In April, though, by day and night
With countless primrose lamps alight);
Where violets bloom, grow pale and die,
And no one ever passes by;
Or I may watch the sunset slopes
Take on what seems that peace, by hopes
And dreams unvexed, for which they pray
Who bear the burden of the day—
Yet if at that hushed evening time
The tor beyond the copse I climb,
And see afar a spirt of steam,
And through the trees an instant gleam
(E'en though the village roofs below
Are smothered in the pink and snow

Of apple bloom, from out whose drifts
The grey sun-smitten church-tower uplifts),
A sense of life estranged, apart,
Awakes in my unquiet heart—
Of having lagged and fallen behind
With dreams renounced and fight declined—
For there across the patchwork plain
With far faint thunder glides the train
That races up past field and down
From Plymouth Tide to London Town.

W. G. Hole

LXXXIV: EARTH'S SECRET

Not solitarily in fields we find
Earth's secret open, though one page is there;
Her plainest, such as children spell, and share
With bird and beast; raised letters for the blind.
Not where the troubled passions toss the mind,
In turbid cities, can the key be bare.
It hangs for those who hither thither fare,
Close interthreading nature with our kind.
They, hearing History speak, of what men were,
And have become, are wise. The gain is great
In vision and solidity; it lives.
Yet at a thought of life apart from her,
Solidity and vision lose their state,
For Earth, that gives the milk, the spirit gives.

George Meredith

It was one of those most distinctive winter days of which we have always a dozen or so in each year. On these days the whole scene over large and wooded English landscapes is presented in brown and yellow. The brown, which is mainly a warm umber or sometimes a hazel tint, is the prevailing earthy colour. The litter of dead oak-leaves in parks and woods, the beaten-down brake fern, the longer and coarser tussocks of dead grass, the stems of oak-trees and of hazel and other mixed underwoods, combine to make this prevailing earth brown more than the brownest of the plough-fields and fallows; and all the commons and wastes, despite their patches of green, add their quota. All through the winter this brown scene is a familiar sight to the eye for English landscape—a great levelling calming sight that powerfully rules the mind.

But days come now and then, extremely clear days despite the film of blue that lies about the not distant trees like a bloom, when the yellow is more signal even than the brown. It arises from the brilliant winter sunshine in which nearly the whole morning and—in February or March—three hours or more of the afternoon are saturated. It never fluctuates, this intense yellow light, but goes on shining and shining without the slightest intermission till, about half-past three or four, it quickly dies out. All through these hours of sombre brown and shining intense gold yellow, one bird sings and sings; and in his note is a mingling of joy and pathos which, I think, is hardly surpassed by any note of Spring—the missel-thrush. Otherwise these brown and yellow days, in large parklands and

commons and beech and oak woods mingled, are
extremely quiet. They are the reflective days of the
year and of human life.

George A. B. Dewar

LXXXVI: OLD MEG

Old Meg she was a gipsy,
    And liv'd upon the moors;
Her bed it was the brown heath turf,
    And her house was out of doors.
Her apples were swart blackberries,
    Her currants, pods o' broom;
Her wine was dew of the wild white rose,
    Her book a churchyard tomb.

Her brothers were the craggy hills,
    Her sisters larchen trees;
Alone with her great family
    She liv'd as she did please.
No breakfast had she many a morn,
    No dinner many a noon,
And, 'stead o' supper, she would stare
    Full hard against the moon.

But every morn of woodbine fresh
    She made her garlanding,
And, every night, the dark glen yew
    She wove, and she would sing.
And with her fingers old and brown
    She plaited mats of rushes,
And gave them to the cottagers
    She met amongst the bushes.

Old Meg was brave as Margaret Queen
  And tall as Amazon;
An old red blanket cloak she wore,
  A chip-hat had she on:
God rest her aged bones somewhere!
  She dies full long agone!

John Keats

LXXXVII: GREEN GROW THE RUSHES-HO

I'll sing you one-ho!
Green grow the rushes-ho.
What is your one-ho?
One is one and all alone
And evermore shall be so.

I'll sing you two-ho!
Green grow the rushes-ho.
What are your two-ho?
Two, two, the lily-white boys,
Clothed all in green-ho,
One is one, etc.

I'll sing you three-ho!
Green grow the rushes-ho.
What are your three-ho?
Three, three, the rivals,
Two, two, etc.

I'll sing you four-ho!
Green grow the rushes-ho.
What are your four-ho?
Four for the gospel-makers,
Three, three, etc.

I'll sing you five-ho!
Green grow the rushes-ho.
What are your five-ho?
Five for the symbols at your door,
And four for the gospel-makers, etc.

I'll sing you six-ho!
Green grow the rushes-ho.
What are your six-ho?
Six for the six proud walkers,
Five for the symbols, etc.

I'll sing you seven-ho!
Green grow the rushes-ho.
What are your seven-ho?
Seven for the seven stars in the sky,
And six for, etc.

I'll sing you eight-ho!
Green grow the rushes-ho.
What are your eight-ho?
Eight for the April rainers,
Seven for the, etc.

I'll sing you nine-ho!
Green grow the rushes-ho.
What are your nine-ho?
Nine for the nine bright shiners,
Eight for the April rainers, etc.

I'll sing you ten-ho!
Green grow the rushes-ho.
What are your ten-ho?
Ten for the ten commandments,
Nine for the, etc.

I'll sing you eleven-ho!
Green grow the rushes-ho.
What are your eleven-ho?
Eleven for the eleven went up to heaven,
And ten for the, etc.

I'll sing you twelve-ho!
Green grow the rushes-ho.
What are your twelve-ho?
Twelve for the twelve apostles,
Eleven for the eleven went up to heaven,
Ten for the ten commandments,
Nine for the nine bright shiners,
Eight for the April rainers,
Seven for the seven stars in the sky,
Six for the six proud walkers,
Five for the symbols at your door,
Four for the gosepl-makers,
Three, three the rivals,
Two, two the lily-white boys
Clothed all in green-ho,
One is one and all alone
And evermore shall be so.

Folk Song

LXXXVIII: TRAMPING AND COLLECTING

Once in a while we have an ideal tramping summer, like that of 1928, when it was much more comfortable to be sleeping out of doors than in a house. It was a great tramping summer. Of course, devotees of walking can tramp happily in the rain, but to get the full pleasure and flavour out of a walking tour one should not have to break it by going to hotels and cottages for meals and beds. You carry a blanket and a pot. Beyond the exhilaration of walking itself, the happiest moments of the day are by the wood-fire in the evening and the wakening in the dawn.

When I was a boy no parents, teachers, friends, or aged relatives would allow us to sleep out, unless it was in the garden, and that was regarded as a fearsome escapade. I remember my father staying up till two in the morning waiting for me to return from a late sugaring expedition, and the glassy expression of his face giving way to relief when he saw me enter with net and poison-bottle and chip-boxes full of drunken moths. I said: " There is another period when the moths come out, just before dawn, and really one ought to stay for that, but I thought I'd better come home." The ideal arrangement would have been to have had a camp in the woods and slept there in those breathless watches of the night when the moths sleep too.

Nowadays, thanks largely to the Scouts, boys have won a great deal of open-air freedom. Mothers can slumber peacefully at home, not thinking that wild beasts are devouring their offspring, or gipsies kidnapping them, or bloodthirsty tramps cutting their throats. So you can sleep out now, and that means that you are free for all sorts of jolly adventures.

I am all in favour of combining some hobby with tramping, preferably natural history: the collecting of butterflies and moths, beetles, birds' eggs, pupæ, wild flowers. If you are already collectors, how you would enrich your collections on a real tramp of a week or a fortnight or more. You don't really find very much indoors, except when you sit with the light on at an open window at night. But in twenty-four hours a day in the open you double or even treble your opportunities.

It is just as well to have a friend, and tramp in twos or threes. It makes it easier to carry what you need, and you must beware of carrying a heap of stuff. The less you carry the better. First night out may be cold, but you will get acclimatised and you will learn to choose protected places for your little camping-grounds. You will discover that it is warmer under a tree than in an open field, warmer in woods than merely under a tree, and sometimes warmest of all on the right side of a hayrick.

You do not need to carry a lot of food, as in England anyway you will generally be able to get what you want for your next meal at some cottage or wayside inn or shop within an hour of when you want to eat it. You carry tea and sugar and matches. You will find a metal coffee-pot better to carry than a kettle. Its spout does not fall off and it is more easily stowed away in knapsack. In that pot you can not only make your tea but boil eggs. A little frying-pan is easy to carry and comes in very useful. If you combine fishing and tramping you will not need to be reminded of the frying-pan. It is just as well to have little cotton bags in which to put tea, sugar, salt, and other things that spill and mix. Sometimes you can buy them at a

Woolworth's, and while there get fork and spoon. You will have your own substantial pocket-knife which can serve many purposes. Wear comfortable boots with thick soles, and then you do not need to carry an extra pair, though a pair of old gymnasium shoes can be a great comfort. You should carry a waterproof or something in the nature of a ground-sheet. You don't need a tie, but you do need an extra pair of stout boot-laces and some string, matches, one or two rags, and an old glove. That glove is to take the pot off the fire when it has got so hot you can't touch it, or to steady it when suddenly you see it toppling over, putting out the fire and spilling your precious tea.

But where will you go? I vote for forests, mountains, or moors. Devonshire is very good; so is the New Forest; if you are a collector you may be tempted once to the Fens, but it is apt to be damp and dreary there. There is the Scottish border; there is the Dorset coast. You can have good bathing at little seaside villages which the ordinary holiday-maker seldom visits. In England and Scotland alone there is an endless variety of possibilities. Step off the great highway rolling with motors and coaches, and you are at once in tramping country. You can trespass a good deal if you don't do damage. Walk at the side of the fields rather than across them. When making your fire don't pull out wood which has been put by farmers into hedges to keep sheep from straying on to the road, don't make fires near haystacks, and in any case don't run away from " old men." If when trespassing you see someone coming toward you, meet him quite cheerfully and politely. In nine cases out of ten he will be friendly. If he does not like you tramping over his property, of course, you will make your exit by the nearest gate. There is plenty more country all around. And remember " a soft answer turneth away wrath," and don't be cheeky.

I am always being asked how many miles I think one ought to do in a day. My answer is that there is no " ought " about it. You do what you can, and what you feel like. At first you will want to overdo it. That is a danger. You are having such fun, no number of miles tires you. It is generally on the second day out that you blister your heels. On the first day you start from home and bed at what is called a reasonable hour. On the second, waking before sunrise, you may make the mistake of getting in a whole day's ordinary walk before ten o'clock, and another whole day's walk before three, and yet another before sunset, three days' tramping in one day. But unless you are in special training you generally get too tired if you do more than thirty miles in a day. Twenty miles is a good stretch, and fifteen miles a day is a good average. If you spend the nights out of doors you will seldom do less than twelve miles. Of course, if you are combining collecting and tramping, distance tramped will hardly count for much. The collector is much more likely to estimate his day's pleasure by the number of his specimens. He may spend hours watching shy birds to find a nest, or he reaches the habitat of a certain insect; he comes to a long gully overgrown with brambles and his eye rests on a larva of an emperor moth, or he comes to a wood where the elusive Hairstreak is dancing among the birch leaves —the entomologist is apt to spend the best part of a day in such places.

An interesting natural history tramp can be begun in late August, go through September and October.

Go pupa-digging! You arm yourself merely with a trowel. You carry a few tin cigarette-boxes filled with moss, and set off to dig in the angles of the trees for moths in their third stage of being—the chrysalis or pupa. You can with ease find hundreds of them. You keep them in light mould or fibre through the winter, and in the spring and early summer of the following year watch the perfect insects emerge, a dozen or so new births every morning. I remember one autumn when I was a boy I dug up five hundred and seventy odd pupæ. A lot of them came from the trees in the fields on the fringes of Dartmoor, and last summer, happening to be in the neighbourhood of Chudleigh, I looked again at some of the trees around whose roots I spent so many happy hours, and especially at one tree where I was watched by an old lady who was fascinated by the strange behaviour of a trespasser, and watched me working away with my trowel in the angle of one of her great oaks.

" I hope you are doing no damage," said she.

" Oh no," said I. " I only dig on the north side of the trees."

" On the north side—how strange! "

" Yes, the larvæ only come down on the north side. That has been discovered by naturalists. So I do not waste time digging on the other sides. It is good for the tree."

I showed her a tobacco-box well filled with Oak Beauties and Prominents, and then I found she thought I was digging bait for fishing.

Pupa-digging strikes some grown-ups as a very astonishing occupation.

If you start a tramp of this kind in August, you will only get the pupæ of the moths that come out in the very early spring, the many visitors to sallow-blossom; but you will probably get Oak Beauties, which most boys prize. It is a large and lovely moth that creeps out of the shell in late March. But in September and October you will get more variety. And different trees yield different species. Don't forget the limes, the poplars, the willows, and the aspens. In a long tramp through southern and western country you will come upon a variety of soils and find species in patches. Once from an avenue of limes I took upwards of sixty lime-hawks. You probably do not want sixty lime-hawks, but it is great fun to watch them come out in the early summer, beautiful, powerful insects that go from your bedroom window away over the tree-tops in the gardens, looking like little aeroplanes taking off.

When tramping from field to field and clambering over stiles and through hedges, one is apt to shake up the contents of those tin-boxes. It is important to have enough moss to keep the chrysalises from knocking against one another. And when counting your spoils avoid touching them with your fingers. Do not try to make their tails twitch in order to be sure they are alive. They are alive all right. But if handled too much the little wings inside the wing-cases will get bruised and never grow to full flying length.

Another jolly sort of long field expedition is the wild-flower collecting tramp. See how many different flowers you can find in three weeks. Before pressing them, look very carefully at them, especially if you do not know their names. You will want to identify them all when you get home, and sometimes it is not so easy to tell just exactly what a pressed blossom looked like when it was alive on its stem.

This is where the notebook comes in. You should always carry a notebook or diary. You can make yourself a diary. There is never enough room in the diary you buy at a shop. While you are on tramp you will need three or four pages a day. That is because you have so many experiences. And if you are collecting, you may need even more space than that to set down names and places and descriptions of the things you find.

I should carry a copying-ink pencil, not a fountain-pen. It is sometimes difficult to get a re-fill, and it is a mistake carrying ink in a knapsack. Ink pellets get lost. Ordinary pencil rubs out. But if you are a botanist and can accompany your notes with drawings of flowers, you will need a fine-point pencil and may even prefer to carry a pen.

A sketch-book or a small camera are both useful on tramp, especially the sketch-book, and even if you cannot draw with any success, you may sometimes draw something for your own amusement, sometimes memorise a scene just by a few rough lines that perhaps mean nothing except to you alone. Sometimes, also, you want to make a little map. You have found a bank where certain uncommon flowers are to be found. You may want to return, or to send others there—well, a map, a little plan has to be made.

Whatever the weather you should try to keep your diary dry. You will keep it in an inside pocket of your coat or in a waterproof-cover in a pocket of the knapsack. Also you must be careful not to leave it behind. When all is packed up and the embers of the fire have been stamped and watered out, there is just one little thing that may be lying overlooked on the grass or behind a rock—it is your notebook.

Sometimes you will be possessed by a passion for scribbling, and fill page after page in your diary. It will be a rainy afternoon, or a long blissful evening by the camp-fire. That is splendid. What pleasure you will have in going over it later when you get home. Though often one's impressions are so unforgettable that it seems scarcely worth while writing them down.

In thinking of where the amateur tramp will spend his night, it is as well not to leave the matter till too late an hour. If you happen to see a perfect spot as early as five in the afternoon it may be just as well to stop there. After five the eyes should be on the alert for " perfect spots." You want a softish bed; a place where there is plenty of wood for the fire; a possible refuge in case of heavy rain. You are on the look-out for trees with really thick foliage, or for an over-hanging bank of earth, or perhaps for a convenient haystack or a barn. Personally I hate barns, and do not like sleeping in messy hay. But—any port in a storm! If it is going to be very wet—well, a barn.

There is a great deal of craft in choosing a place for the night, and it needs more space than I can give. But here are a few suggestions. Do not try to sleep on a slope—you will be rolling and slipping all night. Flat ground can be also uncomfortable; you need to cover it with a lot of heather or bracken or foliage. A slight hollow is best. If the ground is wet and you are on some place like the Yorkshire moors, stub up as much dry dead heather as you can find. Make your bed two foot deep in springy heather, and then put your ground-sheet on top of that, and flop into it. That's the tramp's feather bed. You can sleep happily on that with the mountain mist drifting over you all night, and feel none the worse. You can be quite happy tramping and camping in the wet. Starting your fire is, however, a problem. You should carry dry paper somewhere about you. With that as a foundation you can start a fire even in the wettest surroundings. You must start the fire with the stems of withered weeds and the tiniest tiniest twigs, with dead furze and rusty pine-needles. Do not gather wet wood out of the grass, but break dead wood from trees and the dead thorny stems you always find in briars and the brittle ends of bramble-stalks. Get a blazing short-time fire to dry the wetter stuff, and then that too will burn. And once you've got your fire, especially on a wet evening, keep it going! Get big wood and frame the fire with it, and keep building with small wood. A fire that keeps blazing and hissing in the drizzle is a great triumph and a great comfort. Before going to sleep for the dark hours it is as well to put stones or some old bit of rusty iron or a great lump of wood over the embers, just to keep a place warm and dry as a site for the morning fire.

Morning is perfect. It hardly matters what weather you have. I hope it is by the sea, or by a pond or lake or stream, and that while the blue smoke is coiling upward from the renewed bonfire you can have a morning dip, and come back from it glistening and wet and light-hearted to put the pot in the best place to boil for tea. I am hoping you will not have bad luck and that it will not simply go on raining, day after day. In that case you would do well to try and get a farmer to take you in, just to dry. But out of doors there seems to be more sunshine than one imagines when living under a roof. After a wet night you often get a hot sunny morning. In that case it is wise to dry everything thoroughly before starting further afield. It may cloud over by eleven. But that does not matter if your clothes and blanket and knapsack are dry again.

It is all great fun. I strongly advise you, next summer, to think of tramping. A pair of boots with stout soles, and a heart likewise, a hobby! Open the door, and the world is yours.

LXXXIX

The sky is changed!—and such a change! O night,
And storm, and darkness, ye are wondrous strong,
Yet lovely in your strength, as is the light
Of a dark eye in woman! Far along,
From peak to peak, the rattling crags among
Leaps the live thunder! Not from one lone cloud,
But every mountain now hath found a tongue,
And Jura answers, through her misty shroud,
Back to the joyous Alps, who call to her aloud!

And this is in the night:—most glorious night!
Thou wert not sent for slumber! let me be
A sharer in thy fierce and far delight,—
A portion of the tempest and of thee!
How the lake shines, a phosphoric sea,
And the big rain comes dancing to the earth!
And now again 'tis black,—and now, the glee
Of the loud hills shakes with its mountain-mirth,
As if they did rejoice o'er a young earthquake's birth.

Now, where the swift Rhone cleaves his way between
Heights which appear as lovers who have parted
In hate, whose mining depths so intervene,
That they can meet no more, though broken-hearted;
Though in their souls, which thus each other thwarted,
Love was the very root of the fond rage
Which blighted their life's bloom, and then departed:
Itself expired, but leaving them an age
Of years all winters—war within themselves to wage.

Now, where the quick Rhone thus hath cleft his way,
The mightiest of the storms hath ta'en his stand:
For here, not one, but many, make their play,
And fling their thunderbolts from hand to hand,
Flashing and cast around; of all the band,
The brightest through these parted hills hath forked
His lightnings,—as if he did understand,
That in such gaps as desolation worked,
There the hot shaft should blast whatever therein
    lurk'd.

Sky, mountains, river, winds, lake, lightnings! ye!
With night, and clouds, and thunder, and a soul
To make these felt and feeling, well may be
Things that have made me watchful; the far roll
Of your departing voices, is the knoll
Of what in me is sleepless,—if I rest.
But where of ye, O tempests! is the goal?
Are ye like those within the human breast?
Or do ye find, at length, like eagles, some high nest?

Could I embody and unbosom now
That which is most within me,—could I wreak
My thoughts upon expression, and thus throw

Soul, heart, mind, passions, feelings, strong or weak,
All that I would have sought, and all I seek,
Bear, know, feel, and yet breathe—into *one* word,
And that one word were Lightning, I would speak;
But as it is, I love and die unheard,
With a most voiceless thought, sheathing it as a sword

Byron

XC: DOVER BEACH

The sea is calm to night.
The tide is full, the moon lies fair
Upon the straits;—on the French coast the light
Gleams and is gone; the cliffs of England stand,
Glimmering and vast, out in the tranquil bay.
Come to the window, sweet is the night-air!
Only, from the long line of spray
Where the sea meets the moon-blanch'd land,
Listen! you hear the grating roar
Of pebbles which the waves draw back, and fling,
At their return, up the high strand,
Begin, and cease, and then again begin,
With tremulous cadence slow, and bring
The eternal note of sadness in.

Sophocles long ago
Heard it on the Ægean, and it brought
Into his mind the turbid ebb and flow
Of human misery; we
Find also in the sound a thought,
Hearing it by this distant northern sea.

The Sea of Faith
Was once, too, at the full, and round earth's shore
Lay like the folds of a bright girdle furl'd.
But now I only hear
Its melancholy, long, withdrawing roar,
Retreating, to the breath
Of the night-wind, down the vast edges drear
And naked shingles of the world.
Ah, love, let us be true
To one another! for the world, which seems
To lie before us like a land of dreams,
So various, so beautiful, so new,
Hath really neither joy, nor love, nor light,
Nor certitude, nor peace, nor help for pain;
And we are here as on a darkling plain
Swept with confused alarms of struggle and flight,
Where ignorant armies clash by night.

Matthew Arnold

XCI: SLEEP OF ODYSSEUS

Then Odysseus turned from the river, and fell back
in the reeds, and kissed earth, the grain-giver, and
heavily he spake unto his own brave spirit:

" Ah, woe is me! what is to betide me? what shall
happen unto me at the last? If I watch in the river
bed all through the careful night, I fear that the bitter
frost and fresh dew may overcome me, as I breathe
forth my life for faintness, for the river breeze blows
cold betimes in the morning. But if I climb the hillside up to the shady wood, and there take rest in the
thickets, though perchance the cold and weariness

leave hold of me, and sweet sleep may come over me, I fear lest of wild beasts I become the spoil and prey."

So as he thought thereon this seemed to him the better way. He went up to the wood, and found it nigh the water in a place of wide prospect. So he crept beneath twin bushes that grew from one stem, both olive trees, one of them wild olive. Through these the force of the wet winds blew never, neither did the bright sun light on it with his rays, nor could the rain pierce through, so close were they twined either to other; and thereunder crept Odysseus, and anon he heaped together with his hands a broad couch; for of fallen leaves there was great plenty, enough to cover two or three men in winter time, however hard the weather. And the steadfast goodly Odysseus beheld it and rejoiced, and he laid him in the midst thereof and flung over him the fallen leaves. And as when a man hath hidden away a brand in the black embers at an upland farm, one that hath no neighbours nigh, and so saveth the seed of fire, that he may not have to seek a light otherwhere, even so did Odysseus cover him with the leaves. And Athene shed sleep upon his eyes, that so it might soon release him from his weary travail, overshadowing his eyelids.

Homer

XCII

There goes a wanderer through the night
With lusty gait;
The crooked valley and the height
Upon him wait.
Blithe is the night—
He stands not still, he strides abroad,
He seeketh out his unknown road.

There sings a bird through the night,
" Ah bird, thou hast me in despite!
Why dost thou hold my thought, my feet,
Pourest heart's languishing so sweet
Into my ear, so that I need
Listen and heed—
Why dost thou *tempt* me, dost thou greet? "

The gentle bird was dumb and said:
" Nay, wanderer, nay! be comforted;
My voice is rife
To tempt anear a little wife—
What is't to thee?
Alone is night not fair to me.
What is't to thee? So were it best
Thou go, and never never rest!
Why stay'st thou yet?
How should my mellow music stir
Thee, wanderer? "

The gentle bird was dumb and thought:
How should my flute song tell him aught?
He does not stir,
The piteous, piteous wanderer.

Nietzsche
(Translated by John Gray)

XCIII: ON LYING AWAKE AT NIGHT

" Who hath lain alone to hear the wild goose cry? "

About once in so often you are due to lie awake at
night. Why this is so I have never been able to discover. It apparently comes from no predisposing un-
easiness of indigestion, no rashness in the matter of
too much tea and tobacco, no excitation of unusual
incident or stimulating conversation. In fact, you turn
in with the expectation of rather a good night's rest.
Almost at once the little noises of the forest grow
larger, blend in the bigness of the first drowse; your
thoughts drift idly back and forth between reality and
dream; when—*snap!*—you are broad awake!

Perhaps the reservoir of your vital forces is full to
the overflow of a little waste; or perhaps, more subtly,
the great Mother insists thus that you enter the temple
of her larger mysteries.

For, unlike mere insomnia, lying awake at night in
the woods is pleasant, The eager, nervous straining
for sleep gives way to a delicious indifference. You do
not care. Your mind is cradled in an exquisite poppy-
suspension of judgment and of thought. Impressions
slip vaguely into your consciousness and as vaguely
out again. Sometimes they stand stark and naked for
your inspection; sometimes they lose themselves in
the midst of half-sleep. Always they lay soft velvet
fingers on the drowsy imagination, so that in their
caressing you feel the vaster spaces from which they
have come. Peaceful-brooding your faculties receive.
Hearing, sight, smell—all are preternaturally keen
to whatever of sound and sight and woods perfume is
abroad through the night; and yet at the same time

active appreciation dozes, so these things lie on it sweet and cloying like fallen rose-leaves.

In such circumstances you will hear what the *voyageurs* call the voices of the rapids. Many people never hear them at all. They speak very soft and low and distinct beneath the steady roar and dashing, beneath even the lesser tinklings and gurglings whose quality superimposes them over the louder sounds. They are like the tear-forms swimming across the field of vision, which disappear so quickly when you concentrate your sight to look at them, and which reappear so magically when again your gaze turns vacant. In the stillness of your hazy half-consciousness they speak; when you bend your attention to listen, they are gone, and only the tumults and the tinklings remain.

But in the moments of the audibility they are very distinct. Just as often an odour will wake a vanished memory, so these voices, by the force of a large impressionism, suggest whole scenes. Far off are the cling-clang-cling of chimes and the swell-and-fall murmur of a multitude *en fête*, so that subtly you feel the grey old town, with its walls, the crowded marketplace, the decent peasant crowd, the booths, the mellow church building with its bells, the warm, dust-moted sun. Or, in the pauses between the swish-dash-dashings of the waters, sound faint and clear voices singing intermittently, calls, distant notes of laughter, as though many canoes were working against the current; only the flotilla never gets any nearer, nor the voices louder. The *voyageurs* call these mist people the Huntsmen, and look frightened. To each is his vision, according to his experience. The nations of the earth whisper to their exiled sons through the voices of the rapids. Curiously enough, by all reports, they suggest always peaceful scenes—a harvest field, a street fair, a Sunday morning in a cathedral town, careless travellers—never the turmoils and struggles. Perhaps this is the great Mother's compensation in a harsh mode of life.

Nothing is more fantastically unreal to tell about, nothing more concretely real to experience, than this undernote of the quick water. And when you do lie awake at night, it is always making its unobtrusive appeal. Gradually its hypnotic spell works. The distant chimes ring louder and nearer as you cross the borderland of sleep. And then outside the tent some little woods noise snaps the thread. An owl hoots, a whip-poor-will cries, a twig cracks beneath the cautious prowl of some night creature—at once the yellow sunlit French meadows puff away—you are staring at the blurred image of the moon spraying through the texture of your tent.

The voices of the rapids have dropped into the background, as have the dashing noises of the stream. Through the forest is a great silence, but no stillness at all. The whip-poor-will swings down and up the short curve of his regular song; over and over an owl says his rapid *Whoo, whoo, whoo*. These, with the ceaseless dash of the rapids, are the web on which the night traces her more delicate embroideries of the unexpected. Distant crashes, single and impressive; stealthy footsteps near at hand; the subdued scratching of claws; a faint *sniff! sniff! sniff!* of inquiry; the sudden clear tin-horn *ko-ko-ko-oh* of the little owl; the mournful, long-drawn-out cry of the loon, instinct with the spirit of loneliness; the ethereal call-note of the birds of passage high in the air; a *patter, patter,*

202

patter among the dead leaves, immediately stilled; and then, at the last, from the thicket close at hand, the beautiful silver purity of the white-throated sparrow—the nightingale of the North—trembling with the ecstasy of beauty, as though a shimmering moonbeam had turned to sound; and all the while the blurred figure of the moon mounting to the ridge-line of your tent—these things combine subtly, until at last the great Silence of which they are a part draws you forth to contemplation.

No beverage is more grateful than the cup of spring water you drink at such a time; no moment more refreshing than that in which you look about you at the darkened forest. You have cast from you with the warm blanket the drowsiness of dreams. A coolness, physical and spiritual, bathes you from head to foot. All your senses are keyed to the last vibrations. You hear the littler night prowlers, you glimpse the greater. A faint, searching woods perfume of dampness greets your nostrils. And somehow, mysteriously, in a manner not to be understood, the forces of the world seem in suspense, as though a touch might crystallise infinite possibilities into infinite power and motion. But the touch lacks. The forces hover on the edge of action, unheeding the little noises. In all humbleness and awe, you are a dweller of the Silent Places.

At such a time you will meet with adventures. One night we put fourteen inquisitive porcupines out of camp. Near M'Gregor's Bay I discovered in the large grass park of my camp-site nine deer, cropping the herbage like so many beautiful ghosts. A friend tells me of a fawn that every night used to sleep outside his tent and within a foot of his head, probably by way of protection against wolves. Its mother had in all likelihood been killed. The instant my friend moved toward the tent opening the little creature would disappear, and it was always gone by earliest daylight. Nocturnal bears in search of pork are not uncommon. But even though your interest meets nothing but the bats and the wood's shadows and the stars, those few moments of the sleeping world forces are a psychical experience to be gained in no other way. You cannot know the night by sitting up; she will sit up with you. Only by coming into her presence from the borders of sleep can you meet her face to face in her intimate mood.

The night wind from the river, or from the open spaces of the wilds, chills you after a time. You begin to think of your blankets. In a few moments you roll yourself in their soft wool. Instantly it is morning.

And, strange to say, you have not to pay by going through the day unrefreshed. You may feel like turning in at eight instead of nine, and you may fall asleep with unusual promptitude, but your journey will begin clear-headedly, proceed springily, and end with much in reserve. No languor, no dull headache, no exhaustion follows your experience. For this once your two hours of sleep have been as effective as nine.

Stewart E. White

XCIV: CENTRAL ASIAN STARS

Travelling on the Central Asian plain I remember a steady wind that blew all night long, as if it were engaged on the whole-time job of keeping the starry sky polished and swept. All night the ends of my sleeping-sack flapped in the wind, and I looked through trembling eyelashes at the moonlit snowy peaks of the great mountain wall between the " Table-land of fools " and India.

A wind that came all the way out of the heart of China never ceased to blow, and yet never raised the desert sand. The great wind of the old world was blowing, as it has blown for ages. It blew out of the past, turning the monotonous page of history books, blew out of dreams and legends of forgotten man, as out of the story books of the Caliphs, a wind which arose God knows where, far beyond the trails of the caravans, in the heart of the East.

You lie in a marvellous stillness. The stars become your men and women. You become a man of Chaldea, and the constellations revive. There steals into your heart, and oh, how you needed it, the sweet influence of the Pleiades. Spellbound, you watch a ballet, a story up above. There are men on elephants, and men tending camels, long strings of camels, ropes of camels, gulf streams of camels wending their way out of the South of the Universe into the bleak North. There are jewelled queens and striding harlequins and hesitating dwarfs. There are thirteen-year-old brides, with streaming luminous hair, riding on high-stepping ponies, riding the ways of the dark sky, till bid for by the heroes who come striding along the great ways from Arcturus.

The civilised world has been removed like a table that has been cleared, a table cluttered with papers and dishes. Civilisation has been swept to one side. You cannot see it now; it is far away—indeed, out of your ken entirely. You are reduced to a child—whatever your age. You are a petted child of the universe. You shall be all by yourself in the midst of the world, and the Divine picture-book shall be put in your hands for you to open, to look at, to turn the marvellous page. So you lie there enthralled, with dilated, excited, bright-shining eyes; just you, so many feet by so many, and look up at infinite breadth and infinite depth. What is a cabinet thought about the stars,

> " Whoever looked upon them shining
> Nor turned to earth without repining,"

compared with the rapturous poetic experience of having lived nights with them, reading them in the great open chamber of the Universe!

Stephen Graham

XCV: A SUMMER NIGHT

In the deserted, moon-blanch'd street,
How lonely rings the echo of my feet!
Those windows, which I gaze at, frown,
Silent and white, unopening down,
Repellent as the world;—but see,
A break between the housetops shows
The moon! and, lost behind her, fading dim
Into the dewy dark obscurity
Down at the far horizon's rim,
Doth a whole tract of heaven disclose!

And to my mind the thought
Is on a sudden brought
Of a past night, and a far different scene.
Headlands stood out into the moonlit deep
As clearly as at noon;
The spring-tide's brimming flow
Heaved dazzlingly between;

Houses, with long white sweep,
Girdled the glistening bay;
Behind, through the soft air,
The blue haze-cradled mountains spread away,
The night was far more fair—
But the same restless pacings to and fro,
And the same vainly throbbing heart was there,
And the same bright, calm moon.

And the calm moonlight seems to say:
Hast thou then still the old unquiet breast,
Which neither deadens into rest,
Nor ever feels the fiery glow
That whirls the spirit from itself away,
But fluctuates to and fro,
Never by passion quite possess'd
And never quite benumb'd by the world's sway?—
And I, I know not if to pray
Still to be what I am, or yield and be
Like all the other men I see.

For most men in a brazen prison live,
Where, in the sun's hot eye,
With heads bent o'er their toil, they languidly
Their lives to some unmeaning taskwork give,
Dreaming of nought beyond their prison-wall.
And as, year after year,
Fresh products of their barren labour fall
From their tired hands, and rest
Never yet comes more near,
Gloom settles down slowly over their breast;
And while they try to stem
The waves of mournful thought by which they are
    prest,

Death in their prison reaches them,
Unfreed, having seen nothing, still unblest.

And the rest, a few,
Escape their prison and depart
On the wide ocean of life anew.
There the freed prisoner, where'er his heart
Listeth, will sail;
Nor doth he know how there prevail,
Despotic on that sea,
Trade-winds which cross it from eternity.
Awhile he holds some false way, undebarr'd
By thwarting signs, and braves
The freshening wind and blackening waves.
And then the tempest strikes him; and between
The lightning-bursts is seen
Only a driving wreck,
And the pale master on his spar-strewn deck
With anguish'd face and flying hair
Grasping the rudder hard,
Still bent to make some port he knows not where,
Still standing for some false, impossible shore.
And sterner comes the roar
Of sea and wind, and through the deepening gloom
Fainter and fainter wreck and helmsman loom,
And he too disappears, and comes no more.

Is there no life, but these alone?
Madman or slave, must man be one?

Plainness and clearness without shadow of stain!
Clearness divine!

Ye heavens, whose pure dark regions have no sign
Of languor, though so calm, and, though so great,
Are yet untroubled and unpassionate;
Who, though so noble, share in the world's toil,
And, though so task'd, keep free from dust and soil!
I will not say that your mild deeps retain
A tinge, it may be, of their silent pain
Who have long'd deeply once and long'd in vain—
But I will rather say that you remain
A world above man's head, to let him see
How boundless might his soul's horizons be,
How vast, yet of what clear transparency!
How it were good to abide there, and breathe free;
How fair a lot to fill
Is left to each man still !

Matthew Arnold

XCVI

Now came still Evening on, and Twilight grey
Had in her sober livery all things clad;
Silence accompanied; for beast and bird,
They to their grassy couch, these to their nests
Were slunk, all but the wakeful nightingale.
She all night long her amorous descant sung:
Silence was pleased. Now glowed the firmament
With living sapphires; Hesperus, that led
The starry host, rose brightest, till the Moon,
Rising in clouded majesty, at length,
Apparent queen, unveiled her peerless light,
And o'er the dark her silver mantle threw.

John Milton

XCVII: THE GREAT DIVIDE

We dared not start a descent, so we slept on the top of the mountain. I lay on a narrow ledge and slumbered and waked. And Vachel, who was hypnotised by the abyss, would not lie down for fear he might fall off or might get up in his sleep and jump. So he sat like a fakir the whole night long, looking unwaveringly on one fixed spot.

" Our friends all lie in their soft beds with their heads on pillows of down," I thought, " far away in the valleys and across the plains, in snug comfortable homes, and we lie on rocky jagged edges on the very top of a great mountain, far from human ken."

We seemed as much nearer the stars as we were further away from mankind. Venus was like a diamond cut out of the sun, and she lifted an unearthly splendour high into the sooty devouring darkness of the night. In other parts of the sky the meteors shot laconically in and out as if on errands for the planets. Cold winds ravaged the heights but they did not roar. For the forests were far away. And there was no sound of waters—only the long slow threatening roll and splurge of loose rocks continually detaching themselves from the heights and slipping downward to perdition.

I lay and I lay, and Vachel sat unmoving, and we heard, as it were, the pulse of the world. We did not see humanity's prayers going up to God. We only saw the stars and the night. . . .

" Have courage," says the sun in the evening.

" Have faith," say the stars all the night long.

" You see, I rise again; you will rise," says the sun in the morning. " This way, this way," he says till noon, and " Follow, follow," all the afternoon, and then once more, " Behold! I go. Have courage! " he says in the evening again. And that sets young hearts a-beating, that kindles the poet's flame and enlarges the spirit and makes the way of the world.

That makes us all nomads, all gipsies, all pilgrims. That draws the steps of the willing, and even the unwilling find themselves borne along by a human tide and a sliding sand of time—away to the west and the night and the other country. No one can stay, even if he will. In time all must go, all must follow the sun and cross the Divide and go down the slopes of the unimaginable other side and be with the stars in the long hungry night, the myriads of stars that never do anything else but look down on human souls and ask of us and stare at us and dream of us. The night of stars for all of us, and then with our Father and guide, far o'er these mountains, wan and tired, but gleaming and then resplendent, we lift our eyes to the other country, the dreamed-of, hoped-for country—and it is morning and we are still with the light that we followed yesterday.

Stephen Graham

XCVIII

I felt the world a-spinning on its nave,
    I felt it sheering blindly round the sun;
I felt the time had come to find a grave:
    I knew it in my heart my days were done.
I took my staff in hand; I took the road,
And wandered out to seek my last abode.

Hearts of gold and hearts of lead,
  Sing it yet in sun and rain,
" Heel and toe from dawn to dusk,
  Round the world and home again . . ."

My feet are heavy now, but on I go,
  My head erect beneath the tragic years.
The way is steep, but I would have it so;
  And dusty, but I lay the dust with tears,
Though none can see me weep: alone I climb
The rugged path that leads me out of time—
    Out of time and out of all,
    Singing yet in sun and rain,
    " Heel and toe from dawn to dusk,
    Round the world and home again."

Farewell the hope that mocked, farewell despair
  That went before me still and made the pace.
The earth is full of graves, and mine was there
  Before my life began, my resting-place;
And I shall find it out and with the dead
Lie down for ever, all my sayings said.
    Deeds all done, songs all sung,
    While others chant in sun and rain,
    " Heel and toe from dawn to dusk,
    Round the world and home again."

                                John Davidson

XCIX

The sun, that measures heaven all day long,
At night doth bait his steeds the ocean waves among.

                                Edmund Spenser

C

Quoth Sancho:

I only know that while I am in the arms of sleep I have neither fear nor hope, neither trouble nor glory. Blessed be he that invented sleep: it wraps us round like a mantle. It is the food that appeases hunger, the drink that quenches thirst, the fire that tempers cold, the cold that moderates heat, and, lastly, the general coin that can purchase all things, the balance and weight that equals the shepherd with the king, and the simple with the wise. One only evil has it, as I have heard, which is that it resembles death; for between a man asleep and a man dead the difference is little.

Miguel de Cervantes

CI: THE DYING HOBO

Beside a Western water-tank, one cold December day,
Inside an empty box-car, a dying hobo lay:
His partner stood beside him, with a low and bowed-
down head,
Listening to the last words that the dying hobo said.

" I'm going to a better land, where everything is
bright,
Where hand-outs grow on bushes and you can sleep
out every night:
And you never have to work at all, and never change
your socks,
And little streams of whisky come trickling down the
rocks.

214

Tell all the boys in 'Frisco that my face they'll no
    longer view,
Tell them I've caught a fast freight, and I'm going
    straight on through.
Tell them not to weep for me, no tears in their eyes
    must lurk;
For I'm going to a better land, where they hate the
    word called work.

Hark! I hear her whistling, I must catch her on the fly,
One more scoop of beer I'd like, once more before I
    die."
The hobo stopped, his head fell back, he'd sung the
    last refrain,
His partner took his hat and shoes, and caught the
    east-bound train.

Unknown

CII

A boy's will is the wind's will, and the thoughts of
youth are long, long thoughts.

Henry Longfellow

CIII

Ah, my dear God! though I am clean forgot,
Let me not love thee, if I love thee not.

George Herbert

The Westminster Press
411a Harrow Road
London W.9